20 WAYS TO MAKE EVERY DAY BETTER

20 WAYS TO MAKE EVERY DAY BETTER

Simple, Practical Changes with
Real Results

JOYCE MEYER

FaithWords

NEW YORK · NASHVILLE

FaithWords
Hachette Book Group
1290 Avenue of the Americas, New York, NY 10104
faithwords.com
twitter.com/faithwords

First Edition: April 2017

FaithWords is a division of Hachette Book Group, Inc. The FaithWords name and
logo are trademarks of Hachette Book Group, Inc.

The publisher is not responsible for websites (or their content)
that are not owned by the publisher.

The Hachette Speakers Bureau provides a wide range of authors for speaking events.
To find out more, go to www.hachettespeakersbureau.com or call (866) 376-6591.

Library of Congress Cataloging-in-Publication Data has been applied for.

ISBNs: 978-1-4555-6002-8 (hardcover), 978-1-4555-6001-1 (ebook),
978-1-4789-1851-6 (international trade), 978-1-4555-6003-5 (large print)

Printed in the United States of America

LSC-H

10 9 8 7 6 5 4 3 2 1

I came that they may have and enjoy life, and have it in abundance [to the full, till it overflows].

John 10:10

CONTENTS

INTRODUCTION

"I'm just having a bad day."

I can't tell you how many times I've heard people mutter those words (or muttered them myself). Traffic is backed up, you spill your coffee before you even get a sip, the kids are driving you crazy, the kitchen faucet is dripping, your boss is in a mood, and the car is making that funny noise again. *I'm just having a bad day!*

While there aren't many days when *all* of those things happen at once (thankfully), you and I both know that any *one* of those challenges can test our temperament, pollute our perspective, or hijack our joy. Far too often, we write it off as a "bad day" and give up until tomorrow. *Tomorrow will be better*, we hope, while subconsciously waving the white flag of surrender on today.

But the problem with "bad days" is they tend to pile up—have you noticed that? A bad day becomes a bad week. A bad week becomes a bad month. And before you know it, a bad month becomes a bad year. Many of us spend the last week of every December saying the exact same thing: "I can't wait until this year is over!"

Well, if you can relate to that, if you've ever given up on *today*, waiting for *tomorrow*, I wrote this book for you. You see, I don't believe for one moment that you have to go through life held hostage by your circumstances. It doesn't matter what happens around you, if you've accepted Jesus Christ as your Savior, you have the Spirit of God *within* you. Peace, joy, strength, patience...

it's all yours in Christ. Your hope and happiness is not dependent on the world—the Bible says that *"He Who lives in you is greater (mightier) than he who is in the world"* (1 John 4:4).

Sure, there are going to be tough days when things don't go as planned. We all know what it's like to deal with difficulties over the course of the day. Sometimes it's minor (the interview goes poorly, the baby is teething, you cut yourself shaving), and sometimes it's major (you get laid-off from work, the doctor orders a CT scan, your marriage is in trouble). But *whatever* challenges each day brings, you don't have to let those challenges determine your outlook on life. There are things you can do to make your day better!

Sunny or raining, good report or bad, surrounded by friends or standing alone, on top of the mountain or down in the valley—you can enjoy every day of this life God has given you. It's not about what happens *around* you . . . it's about what is happening *in* you! Your decision on how to react to a circumstance is much more important than the circumstance itself. I am thrilled to tell you that you don't have to just *settle* for a bad day; there are many things you can choose to do that will make your day better! I don't like the feeling of being helpless, and I doubt that you do either; therefore, understanding that I have choices available that can make my day better is very encouraging to me, and I hope it will also be encouraging to you.

In more than forty years of ministry, I've noticed that most people don't even realize they are living lives far short of God's best. They've settled for "good enough" and "Oh well, it could be worse," not realizing that God's will is for their lives to get better and better, shining *"more and more (brighter and clearer) until [it reaches its full strength and glory in] the perfect day [to be prepared]"* (Proverbs 4:18).

Is that you? Is it possible that you've set up camp in the land of "trying to make it through the day," when God wants you to move into the land of "truly enjoying each day"? If you're not sure, let me pose a few questions that might help you:

- Is your happiness each day determined by outside factors: How coworkers treat you? What kind of a mood your spouse is in? Unforeseen challenges or obstacles that appear? Or even the weather?
- Do you sometimes feel like you're on an emotional roller coaster—delighted one day but discouraged the next?
- Do you ever dread the day or week ahead, wondering what might go wrong?
- Is your life—marriage, career, family, relationships—semi-good, but you would like it to be much better?
- Do you sometimes feel jealous of the life someone else has?
- Have you settled far short of reaching your original goal?

If you answered yes to even one of those questions, I'm so glad you picked up this book for two reasons: (1) I know how frustrating those feelings can be (trust me, I've been there), and (2) I know how freeing it can be when you learn how to maximize each day and enjoy God's best. And that's what I believe God is going to do for you!

You see, I know God has something profoundly better for your life. And as you and I go through these pages together, I believe God is going to encourage, instruct, and inspire you to see and experience that better life.

The truth is, God wants you to enjoy your life *every* day. Not just occasionally. Not just when the air is clear and the birds are chirping. And not just on weekends or vacations. Every day is a new day with God on your side...and that's a new chance to enjoy the unique, wonderful, destiny-filled life He has given you.

One of my favorite verses in the Bible is John 10:10, because in that verse Jesus promises, *"I came that they may have and enjoy life, and have it in abundance [to the full, till it overflows]."* This is a life-changing, hope-inspiring Scripture, because it clearly tells us that God doesn't just want us to be alive, He wants us to *enjoy* being alive. He wants us to live with joy—abundant, overflowing joy!

My passion as a teacher of God's Word is to help you learn how to live the life Jesus came to give you. That's why we've titled our television program *Enjoying Everyday Life*, and that's why I'm so very excited about this book! I've divided *20 Ways to Make Every Day Better* into four equally important sections: "When You Awake," "New Steps to Take," "Patterns to Break," and "Before It's Too Late." These sections are meant to systematically take you through your day and show you what God's Word teaches about making that day—and every day—count. I believe you can open any chapter, at any time, and apply the principle in that chapter to immediately make your day better.

So if you're ready to experience a new level of joy, contentment, and excitement about your life, get ready. This is a book full of biblical instruction, practical application, stories to inspire, and helpful observations. When you are done with our time together, I believe you're going to have the tools you need to make every single day of your life better. And instead of muttering, "I'm just having a bad day," you'll be shouting, "I'm having *another* great day with God!"

SECTION I

When You Awake

In the morning You hear my voice, O Lord; in the morning I prepare [a prayer, a sacrifice] for You and watch and wait [for You to speak to my heart].

Psalm 5:3

CHAPTER 1

Have a Conversation with God

To be a Christian without prayer is no more possible than to be alive without breathing.

—Martin Luther

Foundations are important. And they are important for this simple reason: A foundation determines how big, how strong, and how successful something can be.

For example, if you had the opportunity to build the home of your dreams—with a bedroom for each of your kids, several guest rooms so friends and family could come and visit, lots of space for hosting parties, a big enough kitchen for the family to hang out in and chat while you cooked, and, most important, big, big, big closets—you'd have to lay a large enough foundation to accommodate such a home.

First things first. The ground has to be leveled ahead of time, the exact dimensions of the home determined, all the plumbing has to be laid out, and the concrete has to be poured and tested. And guess what? All this has to happen before you can enjoy seeing any of the new home!

Well, the same thing that is true for building the home of your dreams is true for building the life of your dreams. The way you start each day (the foundation you lay) will determine how enjoyable and how successful your day is going to be. You can't expect

> *The way you start each day (the foundation you lay) will determine how enjoyable and how successful your day is going to be.*

to have a day filled with joy, optimism, opportunities, and personal progress if you haven't given yourself the right foundation.

If you wake up grumbling and complaining, you've already set yourself up for failure. If you begin the morning dreading the tasks ahead of you, it's that much harder to be successful. If you laid in bed too long and had to start the day rushing around, frantically trying to get dressed and ready to go, you're probably going to feel stressed-out and running behind schedule all day long. Foundations are important.

This is why the very first chapter in this book is "Have a Conversation with God." It's the foundation for this book...and it can be the foundation for your day. And trust me when I say: A conversation with God every morning is the very best foundation you can lay! As a matter of fact, I have discovered in my own life that the only way I can have a good day is if I take time to have a conversation with God before I begin trying to "do" anything else. Take time to "be" with God before you try to "do" what needs to be done that day. That's what prayer is—a conversation with God! It is a comfortable (nonpretentious) conversation between two friends.

The Gospels tell us much about the miracles, the teachings, and the heart of Jesus, but they don't give us a lot of details about His schedule. But Mark 1:35 is an exception. This verse of Scripture says, *"And in the morning, long before daylight, He got up and went out to a deserted place, and there He prayed."* What an important Scripture! It's a peek into the life of Jesus. Jesus spent time in the morning alone with God and praying. I can't help but think that if it was important to Jesus to start His day conversing with God, it should be important for us, too!

Wait! Before you tell me you are not a "morning person," let me simply say that even if you spend a few minutes conversing with God before you begin anything else, it will bring great blessing to the rest of your day. Then, if you need more time to wake up, or even if you prefer evenings for your "God-time," that is fine, but at least begin with God! Let Him know that you want and need Him and His direction and help for your day and for each thing you do throughout the day.

Talking to God

I think some people don't begin their day talking to God because they don't realize what a great honor and privilege it is to be invited to do so.

I am purposely using the terminology "talk to God" and "have a conversation with God" in this chapter, rather than the word "prayer" exclusively, because that is what prayer is. I think we hear so often that we need to pray that perhaps we tend to over-spiritualize the idea and end up seeing it as something that is a job or an obligation rather than an honor. It doesn't have to be eloquent, or even necessarily long, but trying to live without it is foolish. Prayer is asking God to meet your need or someone else's. It's praising Him and thanking Him. It's about committing things to Him and honestly sharing your worries and concerns with Him. There is no subject off-limits with God—you can talk to Him about anything without the fear of being misunderstood, judged critically, or reproached for your faults.

When we talk to God, we open the door for Him to come into

our day—into our problems and situations—and do what we cannot do on our own. We are actually inviting the power of God into our lives. Talking to God about your life doesn't immediately change your circumstances, but it does change something in you and gives you the strength you need to go through your day with a smile on your face. It helps you believe that you are not alone, and that is important for all of us.

When you pray for others, it changes them. We are usually unsuccessful in changing people, even though they may truly need to be changed, but God is very good at it. I recently read something that was very interesting to me. When we pray for other people, God puts thoughts in their mind, thoughts that they would not have had otherwise! They may begin desiring a change in their behavior or choices and not even realize it is God leading them. When we try to talk people into changing, or try to force them to change, they resent us and often become more determined than ever to stay the way they are. When God talks to someone, He is much more persuasive than we are.

When Dave and I got married in 1967, I had many problems in my soul and behavior from the abusive past I had endured. Dave didn't realize how serious my problems were, or even that I had them. Like many people who get married, we knew very little about each other when we said, "I do." Thankfully, Dave was a man who understood the power of prayer, and instead of trying to talk me into changing my attitudes and the way I behaved, he talked to God about me! He confronted me from time to time about my temper or selfishness, but mainly he was a good example, and he trusted God to do what needed to be done.

He has shared that at times, he became so discouraged that he would take a drive and just cry about the situation. He didn't know what to do, but he believed that God did, so he continued to trust and talk to God. He asked God not only to change me, but to help him be patient and not to give up.

Don't struggle and end up frustrated from trying to make things happen that only God can do. Invite Him into every area of your life and watch Him work. I not only suggest that you have a conversation with God in the morning, but that you continue talking with Him throughout your day. The more you talk to Him, the better your day will be.

Listening for God's Voice

Since a conversation involves talking and listening, I want to encourage you to believe you can hear from God, as well as talk to Him. There are many people who aren't sure if God really speaks to people. They may believe He did in biblical times, but they're uncertain if He still does today. And because of this uncertainty, they wonder:

- Is God really interested in my life?
- Does He care about all the little details and does He want to get involved?
- Can I ask God to help me after all the things I have done that are wrong?

I am happy to tell you from God's Word, and my own personal experience as well as that of others, that God talks, and He will definitely talk to you. But to hear Him, you must be listening.

As a young believer, I went to church for years without knowing that God talks to people. I sincerely loved Jesus, I observed all the religious rules and holidays, and I went to church every

Sunday. I was really doing all that I knew to do at that time. But it wasn't enough to satisfy my longing for God. No matter how many church services I attended, it didn't quench the thirst I had for a deeper fellowship with the Lord. I needed to talk to Him about my past and hear Him talk to me about my future. But at that time, nobody taught me that God wants to be intimately involved in the details of our lives and that He speaks to us in many different ways. No one offered a solution for the dissatisfied feelings I lived with.

Through studying God's Word, I learned that He does want to talk to us and He does have a plan for our lives that will lead us to a place of peace and contentment. I began to see that a relationship with God is about more than doing all the right things and attending all the right events.

> *Good communication is the basis for a good relationship!*

My relationship with God is deeply personal. And communication is an important part of any personal relationship. I think it is fair to say that good communication is the basis for a good relationship!

Not only could I talk to God about everything I was going through, but I could listen and expect Him to speak to me in whatever way He desired. And the same is true for you. If you want to see your life get better, it is essential that you believe that God will speak to you and learn the ways in which He does it.

When I talk about hearing the voice of God, people often ask, "Joyce, how do we hear God? Does He speak to us in an audible voice?" Well, God certainly *can* speak in an audible voice if He wants to (the Bible gives examples of this), but more often than not, God speaks to us in other ways. Let me show you some of the ways God will speak to you:

God will speak to you through His Word.

The number one way God speaks to us is through His Word. That's why it is so important not just to read the Bible, but also to study it. Instruction, promises, hope, direction, examples—it's all there! If you want to hear the voice of God, I encourage you to spend some time each day in the Word. Everything the Bible says is God's Word to you! Yes, it is for everyone, but I urge you to take it as a personal letter to you specifically. When you read it, believe it is God speaking directly to you about His will for your life.

God will speak to you through internal peace.

If you're asking God to help you make a decision, what is the option that gives you the most peace? Many times, it is this peace that is telling you the direction to take. Peace always accompanies God's instruction for your life.

God will speak to you through wisdom and common sense.

One of the most practical ways to hear from God is through wisdom and common sense. Wisdom discerns truth in a situation, while common sense gives good judgment in what to do about the truth. I consider wisdom supernatural because it isn't taught by men but is a gift from God.

God will speak to you through an internal, still, small voice.

When we are born again, we are made alive in our spirit to be sensitive to the voice of God. We hear His whisper and we feel His nudging even if we can't tell where it's coming from. He guides us deep within our heart. He convicts, corrects, and directs us by a still, small voice heard in our spirit.

I often refer to this as a "knowing" deep inside. We simply know what is right to do. We feel a certainty that isn't coming from our minds, but from a deeper place within us.

There are other ways God can speak to us, too. He speaks through other people, through nature, through personal conviction, through your own thoughts, through natural things that happen around us, through circumstances, through sermons, worship songs, Bible-based books—these are just a few of the other ways God speaks to His children. The Bible also shows us that at times, He speaks through dreams or visions. All of these ways that God speaks should agree with His written Word. If God's Word (the Bible) doesn't give us exact instructions about something, we can still find within its pages the nature of God, and knowing that enables us to discern between a message from God and one that might not be from God.

A Two-Way Street

As you can see, having a conversation with God is a two-way street. It's not just telling God all the things you need, and it's not just sitting in silence waiting for something to happen. Prayer is about talking and then listening as you go about your day. And just like any other relationship, talking and listening is crucial if you want to grow closer together.

We begin our journey by talking, and then listening and watching for God to speak. He may not answer you quickly, as people often do, but He will make His will known in due time. I recently heard a powerful man of God say that we learn to hear from God by making mistakes. God doesn't require us to do everything perfectly the first time. If your heart is right and you truly want God's direction, He will continue teaching you until the day comes when someone may ask you, "How can I hear from God?" and you will be able to teach them and pass on what you have learned over the years.

I want to conclude this chapter by strongly recommending that at any time throughout the day, if there is anything that seems to be draining your energy or joy and causing you to want to say, "I'll be glad when this day is over," or "This is just not a good day," stop right then and talk to God about the thing that is robbing you of the good day He wants you to have. You can talk to Him anytime, anywhere, about anything, and He is listening!

Things to remember:

- The same thing that is true for building the home of your dreams is true for building the life of your dreams. The way you start each day (the foundation you lay) will determine how joyful and successful your day is going to be.
- When you talk to God, it should be natural to do so. He is your friend and He is interested in everything about you.
- God still speaks today . . . and He wants to speak to you!
- Having a conversation with God is a two-way street. It's not just telling God all the things you need, and it's not just sitting in silence waiting for something to happen. It is about talking *and* listening.

Suggestions for Putting "Have a Conversation with God" into Practice

- Pour yourself a cup of coffee (or whatever you like to drink) tomorrow morning and spend time talking to God until you finish your cup.
- Talk to God just like you would a friend. Ask questions, share your frustrations, be totally and completely honest.
- Be patient with yourself while you are learning how to listen to and hear from God. Don't feel defeated if you make a mistake. We are His children and it always takes children a while to learn new things.
- Before you go to bed, take some time to reflect on the day. When you do this, you will often see in retrospect how God spoke to you and guided you through the day. You may realize that something you thought to be a *coincidence* or a *lucky break* was actually God speaking.

CHAPTER 2

Dream Big

Hold fast to dreams, for if dreams die, life is a broken-winged bird that cannot fly.

—Langston Hughes

A friend recently told me about a conversation he had with a group of children. His nieces had come over to play with his own kids, so he took them all out for breakfast just to get the rowdy crew out of the house. Over donuts, he asked the elementary-aged kids, "What do you want to be when you grow up?" Without hesitation, the children began excitedly to tell him their answers. *My dream is to be a veterinarian! My dream is to be a video game programmer! My dream is to be a worship leader! A hockey player! A nurse!*

My friend told me, "Joyce, it wasn't the professions that got my attention as much as how each response began—'My *dream* is to be a...'" He hadn't asked them about their dream; he had asked them what they wanted to be. But in true childlike fashion, each child spoke with wonder about their "dream."

When I heard this story, I couldn't help but think about how Jesus encouraged us to become like little children (see Matthew 18:3). Their faith, their sense of wonder, their optimism, and their ability to dream—what wonderful traits to have. Children aren't scarred by failure or burdened by doubt. The exact opposite is true. They are hopeful and excited about their future!

I think one of the best things we can do in order to make every day better is to start dreaming again. Dreaming about what the future can hold. Dreaming about what new things we

> *One of the best things we can do in order to make every day better is to start dreaming again.*

can accomplish with God's help. Dreaming about the exciting, adventurous things God has in store for our lives! Keep in mind, I'm not talking about wishful thinking or daydreaming about what life could have been. I'm encouraging you to do so much more—dream big, bold, faith-filled dreams for your life. God's Word says that He can do much more than we can ever imagine or dream (see Ephesians 3:20).

Setting Daily Goals

Setting daily goals helps us see daring dreams come true. That's because dreams are realized one step at a time...one decision at a time...one goal at a time.

Imagine for a moment that you are a world-class Olympic archer. You've practiced for years, perfecting your craft. When there is a bow in your hand and a target before you, there is no one better than you. You've put in the time. You've practiced for years and years. And now you have an opportunity to showcase your skill on the world stage. You're an expert archer, the best in the world—the gold medal is within your grasp!

But as you step up to compete, the cameras trained on you, your country's hope for an Olympic gold medal resting on your shoulders, an unforeseen problem presents itself: there is no target. You've got your bow in one hand, an arrow ready in the other, but you have nothing to shoot at. Puzzled, you inform the judges,

"Um, excuse me, there is no target. What am I supposed to shoot at?" But the panel of Olympic judges just shrugs at you dispassionately. "Shoot at whatever you'd like," they say. "A target isn't really necessary."

Not wanting to disappoint the millions watching on television or anger the judges assigned to your sport, you pull the arrow back, and with muscles tight and your heart pounding, you shoot the arrow forward... into oblivion. There is no target. There is no measure of success. You have no idea if you've performed well or poorly. *What just happened?*

Obviously, the above scenario is pretty absurd. No athlete would compete in a competition where there is no measure for success. If there is no goal—if there is no target—it is a waste of time to participate. In order for anything to be realized, a goal must be set forth.

I tell you that story because I am amazed at the number of people who begin their day with no goals. They wake up in the morning with no plan for the day. Instead of establishing goals and things they would like to accomplish before the day is over, they just float aimlessly through the day. Like an archer with no target, they have nothing to shoot at, so they don't know if they are winning or losing, succeeding or failing. No wonder they aren't enjoying their day... or their lives.

Goals are essential. It is pointless and even frustrating to have a big dream for your life, or even a small dream for the day, without setting goals on how you expect to see your dreams come true. When you set things before you that you'd like to accomplish, it gives you a sense of purpose and intentionality about your day. It doesn't have to be anything major; even something small like cleaning a certain room of the house, reading a chapter or two of a book, setting up an appointment that you have been putting off—any goal is a worthwhile task. I usually set goals and write them down in my journal each morning, and quite often I have more goals than I will be able to accomplish, but I never let that bother me. I do what I can and then begin again the next day.

I believe that quite often people experience "bad days" simply because they aren't doing anything that gives them a sense of satisfaction. God has not created us in such a way that we can ever be satisfied inwardly with nonproductive lives. Any day in which I feel purposeless is one that I don't enjoy. Even if I purpose to rest all day, at least I know my purpose!

When you set a goal and move with a purpose, good things will happen for you, too. You may not know how everything is going to work out. You may not have all the answers for the day ahead. But if you'll set a goal (or two, or three), you'll be amazed at how helpful it can be in improving your outlook for the day ahead.

As the president of a worldwide ministry, setting and meeting goals for each day is crucial for me. For one thing, goals keep me from becoming overwhelmed by the sheer volume of things that have to be done each day. Setting goals is like setting limits on things, so we don't feel that we have to do everything that needs to be done all at once. It would also be very easy to get distracted if I had no goals—goals keep me focused and help me prioritize my time. Each time I complete a task I had set out to do that day, I have a sense of accomplishment, and that feeling is a reward in itself.

The same can be true for you. Whether you're a stay-at-home parent, a full-time employee, a student, a business owner, or a volunteer, goal setting can keep you alert and focused throughout the day, and it can help you feel more enthusiastic about your day. Those who have no direction in their life rarely feel enthusiastic, because it is difficult to feel passionate and enthusiastic about nothing!

Working Toward Your Dream

John Maxwell says, "A dream without a positive attitude produces a daydreamer. A positive attitude without a dream produces a pleasant person who can't progress. A dream together with a positive attitude produces a person with unlimited possibilities and potential."[1] I love this quote because it is so true. It's one thing to have a dream, but in order to see that dream become a reality, there are accompanying action steps you have to take. And one of those steps is having the right attitude.

I'm sure you've heard the old expression: *Your attitude determines your altitude.* Well, this expression is popular for a reason—it's absolutely 100 percent right! You're never going to be a confident, successful, happy person with a doubtful, defeated, sour attitude. It just doesn't work that way. So the first step to take in order to realize any dream—a new career, getting that degree, a stronger marriage, big things for your children—is to adjust your attitude. When you're tempted to think, *It's going to be too hard. I'll probably fail. I'm too old to start over*, remind yourself that your attitude determines your altitude.

- Instead of, *I can't do it*...choose to think, *I can do all things through Christ!* (See Philippians 4:13.)
- Instead of, *This is impossible*...choose to think, *Nothing is impossible with God!* (See Matthew 19:26.)
- Instead of, *What if it doesn't work out?*...choose to think, *What if it does work out!* (See Hebrews 11:1.)

> *When you change your attitude from pessimism to optimism, from fear to faith, you take important first steps to seeing your dream come true.*

When you change your attitude from pessimism to optimism, from fear to faith, you take important first steps to seeing your dream come true.

There are other steps you'll need to take, too. When you have a dream, there is work to be done. You'll have to plan. There will be sacrifices you'll probably have to make. You'll need to persevere on days when everything in you wants to give up. In other words, anytime you follow a dream God puts in your heart, get ready to do everything in your power to make it happen. And here is the really good news: When your power seems insufficient, God's power takes care of the rest. If you'll do your part, God will always be faithful to do His part. Don't give up on the dream when you feel too weak or incapable; God promises in 2 Corinthians 12:9 (NKJV), *"My grace is sufficient for you, for My strength is made perfect in weakness."*

When I first started ministering, I had dreams of all the people I could help by teaching the Word of God, but it didn't happen overnight. And it didn't happen without a lot of work. Dave and I made plenty of sacrifices. There were many meetings where attendance was disappointing. And there were lots of times when we wondered where the money we needed was going to come from. But rather than give in to discouragement and despair (and trust me, that would have been easy to do), we kept at it. We worked hard doing all we could to obey what we knew God had put in our hearts…and God did what we couldn't. On days when I felt like giving up, an encouraging letter would show up in the mail. When it seemed like we were totally out of money, an unexpected financial gift would come in. When one ministry door would close, an even better door would open. Time and time again, God's grace was sufficient.

The same is true for you. Sure, there is work to do in order to see that dream come to pass, and it will probably take longer than you expected it to. But you're never alone. God is with you, and He promises to give you the strength you need. If you've submitted that dream to God, and if you are willing to do your part to see that dream become a reality, God is going to show up and do what you can't do on your own. That's what grace is—it is God's undeserved favor, and it's the power of God to do with ease what you could never have done on your own. So, when you feel weak or unsure, that's not a bad thing. Remember, God's grace is sufficient for you, and His strength is made perfect in your weakness!

> *If you've submitted that dream to God, and if you are willing to do your part to see that dream become a reality, God is going to show up and do what you can't do on your own.*

Giving Life to Your Dreams

God is not a stagnant God. He never changes, but He *is* always on the move. God wants us to be on the move, too. He created us to have goals and dreams, to be the best we can be for His glory. When God gives you a dream, it's a lot like becoming pregnant: You conceive (think or imagine) a vision of the "new thing" He's planned for you. Now you have to make it through the pregnancy and get to full term to birth the fulfillment of that dream (see Isaiah 43:19).

Ecclesiastes 5:3 says, *"For a dream comes with much business and painful effort."* I'm sure this is why many people give up on their dreams somewhere along the way. When they find out it will take effort, be costly and uncomfortable to complete their preparation for the birth of that dream, they conclude it wasn't really God's will after all and go and do something else. I want to encourage you to press through the hard part, because if you give up, you will never be completely satisfied. There will be a part of you that doesn't feel settled or fulfilled. God doesn't make everything in life easy for us, because we grow in the struggle. Faith becomes stronger as we are required to use it.

So how do we successfully make it through preparation and give birth to our God-given dreams? Here are three keys to help you get there.

1. Believe that God is working... and remain spiritually active.

Whatever dream God has put in your heart, stand in faith, believing He can bring it to pass. Each day, as you pursue the promise He has given you, make it a habit to say, "God's working!" You may not know all the details of how it is going to work out, but that's okay. God knows everything from the beginning to the end (see Isaiah 46:9–10). He is in control, and He can bring it to pass!

> Each day, as you pursue the promise He has given you, make it a habit to say, "God's working!"

Resist the trap of falling into a passive attitude that says, "Well, we'll just see what happens." You weren't created to be a passive "we'll see what happens" kind of person. Instead, you can be spiritually active, even when you feel you are in a season of waiting on God. Praying, believing, making faith-filled declarations, seeking God for direction—these are all action steps. And those action steps offer great reward. David said in Psalm 27:13, *"[What would have become of me] had I not believed that I would see the Lord's goodness in the land of the living!"*

True waiting on God is never a static, passive place where you're doing absolutely nothing. You may be waiting physically, but you can stay spiritually active, seeking God's direction and putting your belief and trust in Him, actively recalling to mind your dream on a daily basis.

2. Refuse to give up.

It's easy to start a process—or to have a dream—but it is much more difficult to see it through. That's why so many people's lives fall far short of God's best. They start to obey God, or they start to move in the direction of their dream, but when times get tough or they become weary of waiting, they turn around and run in the other direction.

I want to encourage you today to keep going. Don't be stopped by the circumstances that make it look impossible. Don't pay attention to the "friends" or family members who tell you you're better off not getting your hopes up. Dreams are never reached without struggle. If you'll determine to be a person who keeps moving forward—even if

Dreams are never reached without struggle.

it's just one tiny step a day—you are going to experience a whole new level of joy when that dream is realized. Hang in there! Keep going! Refuse to give up!

3. Realize your dream is about more than you.

Many times people dream of things only for them—what they want out of life, or what's best for only them. But Jesus, our example of how to live, gave His life for the benefit of others. Shortly before He was crucified, He prayed to His Father, *"Not My will, but [always] Yours be done"* (Luke 22:42). Everything Jesus did, He did for us.

To really live the dream God has for us, we need to have a "not my will, but [always] Yours be done" kind of attitude. When we submit our dream to God, asking what He wants to do in us and through us, *that's* when our dreams become bigger than anything we could have imagined. God's plan for your life is nothing to be afraid of. He wants better things for you than you could ever want for yourself. So ask Him to give you a dream that will bless not only your life but the lives of others, too.

Welcome to the Club

The Bible is full of big dreams and daring dreamers. Of course, we know that on many occasions God spoke to men and women through literal dreams, but I like to think of the dreams that heroes of the Bible must have carried in their hearts:

- After being anointed by Samuel, and while tending his father's sheep, David must have dreamed about what it would be like to be king.
- While wearing a coat of many colors, Joseph must have dreamed about what the favor on his life could mean.
- Pregnant with the chosen Messiah, Mary must have dreamed about the upcoming joys of motherhood.

- Traveling on ships from city to city, Paul must have dreamed about what the early church could become.

Dreaming big dreams is part of our spiritual DNA. It's rooted in hope and fueled by faith. God doesn't just *allow* us to dream...
He created us to dream, and to dream big, think big, imagine big, and make big plans. When you begin to do this, you will add excitement to any day.

> God doesn't just allow us to dream...He created us to dream.

So let me encourage you: Dare to dream. Dream about where God can take you. Dream about what God can teach you. Dream about how God can change your situation. Dream about how high you can go and how many people you can help. If you start dreaming, your joy will increase. And if you're worried it might be too hard to dream big, I promise you, it's not...even children can do it.

Things to remember:

- You're never too old to have a dream for your life. Allow yourself to have a childlike optimism for the future.
- There are action steps to take in order to see a dream come true. Don't stand by, passively wishing a thing will happen. Be willing to do the necessary work.
- In order to succeed, it's crucial to have a goal—a target to aim for.
- A big part of seeing a dream come true is simply refusing to give up until it does.
- The Bible is full of men and women who dreamed big dreams for God. Follow their example and dream of what God might do in your life.

Suggestions for Putting "Dream Big" into Practice

- Write out your dream (or dreams) and display it somewhere in your home or office where you will see it every day.
- Take an action step…even if it is a small one. Do something to get the ball rolling with your dream. Call and inquire about taking a class. Read a book that will inspire you. Talk with someone who has been where you want to go. Whatever it may be, just take a first step.
- Start a "dream journal" and fill it with ideas that require big faith. Every time one of these dreams becomes a reality, celebrate. Celebrate God's goodness, knowing that if God did it before, He can do it again!
- Use this acronym when setting your goals tomorrow:

  Get direction from God.

  Order your conversation in line with the dream you have in your heart.

  Avoid people or things that will hinder your progress.

  Leave yourself room for relaxation and downtime.

  Sincerely enjoy trying to accomplish your goals.

CHAPTER 3

Decide to Help Others

No one is useless in this world who lightens the burdens of another.

—Charles Dickens

You may not have heard of General William Booth, but I'm quite sure you've heard of the Salvation Army. Well, it was General Booth and his wife, Catherine, who started the Salvation Army over 150 years ago. The Salvation Army was founded in 1865 as an army of volunteers who would bring salvation to the poor, destitute, and hungry by meeting both their physical and their spiritual needs. It's a mission the Salvation Army still carries out today in 127 countries around the world.

Let me share a story about General Booth that I came across recently:

> It was Christmas Eve, 1910. General William Booth, the founder of the Salvation Army in London, England, was near the end of his life. His health was poor, and he was going to be unable to attend the Army's annual convention. Booth had become an invalid, and his eyesight was failing him. No one knew that he would not live to see another Christmas.

Somebody suggested that General Booth send a telegram or a message to be read at the opening of the convention as an encouragement to the many soldiers of the Salvation Army that would be in attendance following Christmas and their many hours of labor ministering to so many others through the holidays and the cold winter months. Booth agreed to do so.

Knowing that funds were limited and desiring not to use any more money than necessary so that as much money as possible could be used to help the many people in need, General Booth decided to send a one word message. He searched his mind and reviewed his years of ministry, looking for the one word that would summarize his life, the mission of the Army and encourage the others to continue on.

When the thousands of delegates met, the moderator announced that Booth would not be able to be present because of failing health and eyesight. Gloom and pessimism swept across the floor of the convention. Then, the moderator announced that Booth had sent a message to be read with the opening of the first session. He opened the telegram and read the one word message:

Others![2]

General William Booth understood something that many people today have yet to comprehend—there is joy in helping others and profound peace that comes when we put the needs of other people ahead of our own. It is clear that he took Jesus' words to heart: *"It is more blessed (makes one happier and more to be envied) to give than to receive"* (Acts 20:35).

I titled this chapter *"Decide to Help Others"* because when we are not having a great day ourselves, we rarely *feel* like helping someone else. Our tendency is to focus on ourselves. But that is actually the worst thing we can do, because it increases our misery instead of eliminating it.

I am sure that some of you may be thinking, *Joyce, helping another person is great for them, but how can it make me feel better?* I am glad you asked. Let me give you an example that I think you will understand.

What is the best part of Christmas morning or a birthday celebration? It's not when you get to open *your* presents (as nice as that may be). The best part of the morning is when you watch with anticipation as the people in your life open the gifts you've given them. Whether it's a friend, your spouse, your children, or your grandchildren, there is just something wonderful about seeing the joy your gift brings to their faces. You took the time to think about what they would like, made an effort to find it online or in a store, carefully wrapped the gift, and now you get to see how excited they are to receive what you sacrificed to give them.

Well, you can experience that feeling of joy and satisfaction more than one or two times a year. You can experience it every day! When you decide to help others, you're not only going to improve their lives, you're going to improve your own. I guess you could say that one of the best ways to make every day better can be summed up in one word: *Others!*

> When you decide to help others, you're not only going to improve their lives, you're going to improve your own.

The Paradox of the Gospel

The Kingdom of God is made up of paradoxes, things that seem self-conflicting or counterintuitive. In other words, society tells us to do one thing in order to succeed, but the Word of God often instructs us to do the exact opposite. Here are some examples:

- The world tells us to push our way to the front of the line or to the top of the ladder if we want to be first. But the Bible tells us that *the last will be first, and the first will be last* (Matthew 20:16 NIV).
- The world tells us to be stingy and greedy in order to have enough. But the Word of God tells us that when we give, *it will be given to you: good measure, pressed down, shaken together, and running over* (Luke 6:38 NKJV).
- The world tells us to hate our enemies and to hold grudges. But the Word of God tells us to *love your enemies and to pray for those who persecute you* (Matthew 5:44 NIV).
- The world tells us to promote ourselves and to boast about our accomplishments in order to be considered great. But the Bible says that *the greatest among you will be your servant* (Matthew 23:11 NIV).
- The world even says that if we don't take care of ourselves, nobody else will, but the Bible tells us that *a man reaps what he sows* (Galatians 6:7 NIV). And if we sow into other people's lives, then God will bring a harvest of good things into ours (see Galatians 6:8).

As a matter of fact, the promises that God makes to those who reach out and help others are quite amazing. I want you to consider these Bible verses:

> Blessed (happy, fortunate, to be envied) is he who considers the weak and the poor; the Lord will deliver him in the time of evil and trouble.

The Lord will protect him and keep him alive; he shall be called blessed in the land; and You will not deliver him to the will of his enemies.

The Lord will sustain, refresh, and strengthen him on his bed of languishing; all his bed You [O Lord] will turn, change, and transform in his illness.

Psalm 41:1–3

I see at least nine different promises in these three verses of ways we can expect to benefit when we decide to help others. Surely, doing so will improve any day and make it better!

As you can see, the Kingdom of God gives us different instructions than the world gives. And God's way of living is far better, with accompanying heavenly benefits, than the world's way of doing things. This is why God says in Isaiah 55:9, *"For as the heavens are higher than the earth, so are My ways higher than your ways and My thoughts than your thoughts."*

Another one of those paradoxes is the instruction I mentioned at the beginning of this chapter: *"It is more blessed (makes one happier and more to be envied) to give than to receive"* (Acts 20:35). At first glance, it doesn't seem to make sense, does it? How could I be "more blessed" when I am giving, helping, or serving another? It seems like they would be "more blessed" and I would be "more tired." But the truth is much different. When you decide to help others, you yourself are helped.

I can't tell you how many times I have seen this truth work in my own life. There was a time in my life when I was a very selfish person. I had a great deal taken from me throughout my childhood, and I didn't have anyone to protect me. My father abused me for years and my mother knew about it and did nothing to stop it. So you can imagine that later in life,

I thought I had to look out for myself. My thoughts and my actions were all about me. I didn't realize it for a long time, but this self-focus was causing me to be very miserable. All I could think was how unhappy "I" was, and I expected others to make my life better.

But the Lord began to show me that my focus on self was stealing my joy. All I was thinking about was what I *didn't* have or how others *weren't* helping me. When I changed my attitude and started thinking about the blessings I already had and the ways in which I could go out and help others, my outlook on life began to change. I started doing little things on a regular basis to help family, friends, and even strangers...and I discovered it was fun doing it!

The same can be true for you. You can make any day better when you take your focus off of self and begin looking for ways to help and serve others. And you'll be amazed at how much better each day will be. Rather than complaining about your problems or your terrible day, you'll be contemplating how to solve someone else's problems and brighten their day.

> *When you take your focus off of self and begin looking for ways to help and serve others, you'll be amazed at how much better each day will be.*

It's a revolutionary new outlook on life that will bring the peace and joy that only God can give.

Be Adaptable

Most selfish people want their own way, and I was certainly no different. One of my prerequisites for enjoying the day was to have things go the way I wanted them to, but thankfully God taught me how much misery can be relieved by simply adjusting or adapting to a situation or another person.

Learning to adapt and adjust brings peace, and peace leads to joy. This change didn't happen overnight in my life (and it won't in yours either). It was a process that took time. I still like getting my way, but at least now I can adapt if what I want is not happening. I have learned it is one of the ways to stay happy, and I am committed to being happy and enjoying my life. I wasted too many years being unhappy, and I refuse to waste any more.

Today I am practicing being adaptable. Like most married couples, Dave and I don't always like the same things. For example, we like different types of movies, and at times we would choose different restaurants. So I told Dave that tonight I would be happy to let him choose a movie for us to watch and a restaurant for us to eat at. I knew when I did it that I might not like his choices, but if we are going to stay adaptable, we will need to practice doing it. What or who can you adapt to today and perhaps improve the quality of your day?

We can learn how to show love in different ways to different people. Not all people need the same thing from us. One of our children, for example, may need more of our personal time than the others. One of our friends may need more encouragement on a regular basis than another.

For example, all of my family members need me, my employees need me, my friends need me—and they all need me in different ways. Do I ever feel *too* needed? Of course! We all feel overly busy from time to time. But I remind myself that God gives me grace for whatever He places in my life, and I'm fortunate to be loved and needed by so many. When I choose to look at it this way, I get a better perspective—it makes me excited about the

> *Just telling people, "I'm here to help" is not enough. We need to go beyond the words and actually do something to help meet their needs.*

opportunity to serve those around me. After all, just telling people, "I'm here to help" is not enough. We need to go beyond the words and actually do something to help meet their needs.

My husband, Dave, loves to play golf, so I make an effort to ensure that our schedule gives him opportunities to do so. But there was a time when it really bothered me when he would go play golf. I was miserable because I hadn't learned to make room for his needs or desires. I wanted *him* to make all the adjustments. I never acknowledged the many ways in which Dave adjusted to my needs. I never saw what he *did* do—only what he *didn't*—and it was causing me to be unhappy and negatively affecting our relationship. I'm glad that I've learned to adapt and adjust. It didn't happen right away—it was a process—but it greatly improved our marriage. I have also found that since I enjoy seeing Dave enjoy himself, he seems to do more for me than ever. After fifty years of marriage, our relationship is more wonderful than ever.

Once you've decided to be a person who helps others, you'll have no trouble building and maintaining strong, healthy, enjoyable relationships with others. Your primary goal in life will be to put the wishes of others before your own. And when you do that, you'll find that God will fill your life with peace, satisfaction, and incredible joy!

The Not-So-Secret Secret

Deciding to help others is more than a good idea; it is one of the biggest secrets to enjoying every day of your life. People seem

to try everything else first, never realizing the power of living selflessly. But as
believers, you and I really shouldn't be
so surprised by the life-giving results
of putting others first. I can say with
all certainty that learning how to purposely bless others has added more joy

> Deciding to help others
> is more than a good
> idea; it is one of the
> biggest secrets to
> enjoying every day of
> your life.

to my daily life than most other things. One of the things God
taught me was to listen to what people said, and when I did, I
found they usually tell us in conversation what they need, want,
or enjoy. I was at the doctor's office the other day, and the doctor
mentioned a couple of times how much she liked my earrings, so
when I left, I gave them to the nurse and asked her to wait until
I was gone and then give them to the doctor. I won't see her for
another three months and have no way of knowing whether my
gift made her happy or not, but I do know that it made me happy.
There are hundreds of little things like this that we can do to help
others, so there is no excuse for any of us to say, "I don't know
what to do," or "I don't have anything to give."

I believe selfishness is instigated by the devil and that we must
fight it, otherwise it will rule our lives and hinder any hope of
enjoying life. The way to fight it is by deciding to aggressively help
others!

The Bible is full of examples of men and women who put the
needs of others ahead of their own. Let me remind you of a few:

When the land couldn't "nourish and support" the herds of
both Abram and his nephew Lot, Abram selflessly gave Lot the
first choice of the land. Abram said, *"Let there be no strife, I beg of
you, between you and me, or between your herdsmen and my herdsmen, for we are relatives. Is not the whole land before you? Separate
yourself, I beg of you, from me. If you take the left hand, then I will go*

to the right; or if you choose the right hand, then I will go to the left" (Genesis 13:8–9).

Lot was not nearly as selfless. He immediately chose the more fertile land of the east, leaving Abram the inferior territory. But God saw how Abram put his nephew first, and He blessed Abram with tremendous increase. Abram continued to prosper, as opposed to Lot, who fell into great trouble. Abram's kindness and generosity were greatly blessed!

1 Kings 17 tells us the story of the widow in Zarephath, who gave food and water to the prophet Elijah. Keep in mind, there was a famine in the land and this widow had only enough food left for one meal. She was planning on cooking this last meal for herself and her son, and then she assumed they would die. Elijah came on the scene in verse 10 and, at God's instruction, asked the widow for some food and water.

It would have been understandable for the widow to refuse Elijah's request. No one would have thought less of her if she had been unwilling to give away her last meal. But this woman put the needs of Elijah first. She gave him the food and water he requested… and that's when the miracle happened. From that day forward *"the jar of meal was not spent nor did the bottle of oil fail"* (1 Kings 17:16). These were cooking ingredients—they never ran out! From the day she put Elijah first until the famine was over, God miraculously provided everything she and her son needed!

I can't help but think of the relationship between David and his best friend, Jonathan. 1 Samuel 18:1 says that *"the soul of Jonathan was knit with the soul of David, and Jonathan loved him as his own life."*

If you've read the story, you remember that Jonathan was the son of King Saul and was next in line for the throne. But God had other plans. Instead of anointing Jonathan, God sent the prophet Samuel to anoint David to be the next king of Israel. Jonathan could have been jealous, bitter, and angry. He could have resented David and done everything he could to undermine David's rise to the throne. But Jonathan did the exact opposite. When King Saul devised a plan to kill David, Jonathan put David's needs ahead of his own. He warned David of the impending danger and even helped him escape. Jonathan's example of friendship and loyalty is a model that we still read and study today. He is the perfect example of someone who puts the needs of another ahead of his own!

The list doesn't end with those three stories...it's just the beginning: The four men who carried their paralytic friend to Jesus (Mark 2:3); Jacob serving Laban an additional seven years for the hand of Rachel (Genesis 29:27); Jesus washing the feet of His disciples (John 13:4–5); Paul and Silas ministering to their jailor, rather than escaping when the opportunity arose (Acts 16:23–32)—the list of biblical examples of self-sacrifice goes on and on.

With that in mind, it's time we come to understand and embrace the "not-so-secret" secret: Following the biblical model of putting others ahead of yourself is one of the best things you can do to enjoy every day of your life. Whether it's something small, like helping a friend run an errand, or something bigger, like

> *When "others" becomes your first thought, joy will be your new reality.*

volunteering a day of each week to serve the less fortunate in your community—it's all important. It's all life-changing! When "others" becomes your first thought, joy will be your new reality.

Things to remember:

- When you decide to help others, you'll discover how true the words of Jesus are when He said, *"It is more blessed (makes one happier and more to be envied) to give than to receive"* (Acts 20:35).

- The Kingdom of God is made up of paradoxes, things that seem self-conflicting or counterintuitive. Finding the joy in putting others before yourself is one of those.
- Being adaptable is a key to being truly happy.
- The Bible is full of examples of men and women helping others. It's more than just a good idea; it's a biblical model of right living.

Suggestions for Putting "Decide to Help Others" into Practice

- Before you take action, take a little time to simply observe those around you. What are their needs? Who can you help? How can you be most effective?
- Buy a pack of encouraging cards or motivational stationery and leave notes for friends, family, and coworkers.
- Call someone today that you haven't talked to in a while and tell them you were thinking about them and how much you appreciate them.
- Set a goal to make at least three people smile today by giving them a sincere compliment.

CHAPTER 4

Reexamine Your Expectations

Wait and hope for and expect the Lord; be brave and of good courage and let your heart be stout and enduring. Yes, wait for and hope for and expect the Lord.

Psalm 27:14

I want to tell you a little bit about three people we'll call Nancy, Sean, and Lisa. As you read their stories, ask yourself which one of these well-intentioned people you relate to most.

Let's start with Nancy. She is a devoted wife and a loving mother of two beautiful children. She goes to church each weekend, volunteers in the local school system, and shuttles the kids from school to piano lessons to soccer practice most weeknights. By all outward appearances, Nancy has a great life without a care in the world. But nothing could be further from the truth.

In reality, Nancy isn't nearly as happy as her circumstances suggest. She wakes up each day with a sense of dread, wondering what could possibly go wrong today. *Is today the day my husband will lose his job? Is today the day one of my kids will get hurt at soccer practice? Is today the day the doctor will call with terrible news?*

You see, there is something I failed to mention about Nancy. Nancy had a very difficult childhood. Her father left when she was young and her mother remarried and divorced several times. As a child, Nancy dealt with a lot of pain and disappointment.

She grew accustomed to the money running out, the new stepdad taking off, and the other kids at school making fun of her thrift shop clothes. She learned early on in life to expect the worst, and those expectations have followed her into adulthood. Now, instead of enjoying her life and hoping for the best, she spends her days dreading the worst. Nancy should be happy...but she isn't.

Now let me tell you about Sean. He is a single, hardworking young professional who stays busy. When he's not working, he's usually at church or out spending time with his friends. Though he's a very social person, Sean is often frustrated with many of the people in his life. He expects a lot of them. When he's had a bad day, he assumes his friends will encourage him and lift his spirits. When he completes an assignment at work, he craves a pat on the back from his boss. When he needs advice, he assumes the members of his Bible study group will have the perfect words of wisdom. But too many times, those things don't happen. He feels as if people keep letting him down, and he doesn't know what to do about it. Sean should be enjoying the many friends in his life...but he isn't.

Now, before you get too discouraged, let me tell you about Lisa. She is the single mother of three children—one is grown and the other two are progressing through their teenage years. Lisa has gone through her fair share of struggles in life, but she learned a long time ago that she is not defined by the circumstances she has been through. She wakes up each day with hope. She doesn't know what the day is going to hold, but she is confident that God is in control, and that gives her great hope for the events to come.

Though Lisa deals with tremendous pressure at work and comes home to the daunting task of raising teenagers each night, she chooses not be overwhelmed. Rather than living with worry or anxiety, she makes the daily decision to trust God. Instead of letting her job or the demands of others dictate her pace of life, she takes time each morning to ask God what He wants from her that day. Don't get me wrong, Lisa is not perfect; she makes mistakes more often than she would like. But she is committed to asking for God's guidance and living with a calm assurance that He has a purpose and a plan for each day of her life. Lisa has learned the secret of making every day better; she has learned to put her expectations in God and His goodness, instead of in her friends, or even in her circumstances. God created Lisa, like all of us, to live an abundant, overcoming, joy-filled life . . . and she is!

So, let me ask you: Are you more like Nancy, Sean, or Lisa? Nancy has learned to expect the worst. She lives each day with a level of worry, fear, and even dread. Sean, on the other hand, expects a lot of other people . . . maybe too much. He looks to other people to fill the needs in his life, rather than going to God with those needs. Lisa, however, is a different story. She has learned to live with balance. Rather than leaning on her past or looking to others, she begins each day asking God what He wants for her that day. It hasn't been easy, but life has taught Lisa the importance of reexamining her expectations.

If you relate more to Nancy or Sean, don't be discouraged. For many years I was the same way. That's why, when I started working on the outline for this book, I knew I had to include a chapter on expectations. Negative and false expectations are both enemies that work to steal your joy. But if you can learn to place your expectations in God, and adjust them to line up with His good purpose and plan for your life, it's amazing how quickly and effectively it can improve your life on a daily basis. If you see a

> *Negative and false expectations are both enemies that work to steal your joy.*

little bit of Nancy or Sean in your life, keep reading. This chapter can set you in a whole new direction. You see, when people don't do what we expected, and our circumstances don't turn out as we expected, we can still place our expectations firmly in God, trusting that we'll see His goodness in our life.

Refusing to Expect the Worst

Sometimes when you've had a long series of painful or disappointing things happen, you can get to a point where you are just expecting more of what you've already had. Like Nancy, you've been through a lot of trouble and you're simply waiting for more to come. I used to be like that, but I've discovered that God has a better way for us to live.

After surviving a childhood where my father abused me regularly, I married the first guy who came along. I was still a teenager and didn't know any better. The sad thing is, my first husband was a bigger mess than I was. After I was mistreated and abandoned by him, our marriage ended. By the time I met Dave, I was angry and hopeless about everything, just trying to make it through each day.

I had begun to expect the worst all of the time because of the pain I had endured in my life. Even after I had a strong relationship with God, I still struggled with this for a while. Then one morning God brought to my attention how negative my expectations were. I lived with a low level of dread, and was prepared mentally to expect and accept disappointment daily.

Proverbs 15:15 says, *"All the days of the desponding and afflicted are made evil [by anxious thoughts and forebodings], but he who has a glad heart has a continual feast [regardless of circumstances]."* Instead of being a person with a "glad heart," I had become someone who was ruled by "anxious thoughts and forebodings." No wonder I had bad days one after another! Once I read that verse, I began to realize I was dealing with the fear of something bad happening, even when nothing was going wrong. Then I looked back and saw how it had affected me at different times in the past. For example, the night Dave asked me to marry him, he said he needed to talk to me. My response was worry and fear because I thought he was going to break up with me. I was following my usual pattern of expecting the negative. I remember my father saying often during my childhood, "You can't trust anybody. Everybody is out to get you." I now realize he thought that because that was the way he was, but at the time, I allowed his negative attitude to program my mind for the future. Thank God that His Word can renew our minds and we can see His goodwill come to pass in our lives (see Romans 12:2).

When I was expecting something bad to happen, my expectation was actually stealing my happiness. But when I learned to hope for and expect good things, it opened the door to God's plans in my life (see Lamentations 3:25). I would like to suggest that the next time you are having a bad day, examine your expectations, and if you find they are not what they should be, you can quickly make an adjustment that will bring joy back into your life.

If you can relate to my story, I want you to know that God has nothing but incredibly good plans in store for you. He is a good Father who has a great plan for your life. Jeremiah 29:11 (NIV) says it this way: "*'For I know the plans I have for you,' declares the Lord, 'plans to prosper you and not to harm you, plans to give you hope and a future.'*" That doesn't mean that we never have any disappointments or struggles in life, but it does mean that if we keep our expectations in God and His goodness, we will eventually see the good plans He has for us come to pass.

Don't Expect from People What Only God Can Give

If we are going to go through life expecting things, it should only be from God that we expect the best. Any other expectations could just lead us to disappointment and frustration. This is why it is important for us to reexamine our expectations, making sure that our expectation, hope, and trust is in God, not in a person who can let us down. It's not that you can never trust people—the key is to ask God for what you need and then trust Him to work through whom-

> It's not that you can never trust people—the key is to ask God for what you need and then trust Him to work through whomever He chooses.

ever He chooses. God does work through people, but when He is your source, you'll never be disappointed. God may not give you exactly what you are expecting, but He will definitely give you what is best.

Like most people, I spent many years expecting people to keep me happy, meet my needs, and never disappoint me. I had unrealistic expectations, and the result was that I pressured people to do things for me that they often were not able to do. No one can give us a sense of true confidence and self-worth except God, and until we learn to look to Him to meet our needs, we are setting ourselves up for regular disappointment. Are you perhaps angry even now with someone who didn't do what you expected them to? How many days have you spent unhappy and disgruntled because someone didn't do what you expected that they should do? I am ashamed to even think of how high the number is for me.

If you want to make this day, or any day, better, perhaps you should reexamine your expectations and see if they are misplaced. Then if they are, you can change by always looking to God first and foremost for all your needs.

People usually don't mean to hurt or disappoint us, but the truth is, people will let you down from time to time, simply because we are all imperfect. We all have weaknesses. Every person you encounter has a level of selfishness, and many people tend to do what is best for them instead of what is best for other people. We don't have to get angry or bitter with people when they act selfishly; we simply need to look to God for our sense of peace or happiness, not people. As we mature spiritually, we learn that while friends and family can be a great source of encouragement, they can never replace God as our true source of confidence, joy, and strength.

When You Ask God for Help...He Says, "Yes!"

When you just read this section title, you may have thought, *That isn't true, and I'm unhappy today because I did ask and He has not said yes yet!* Just because God doesn't give us what we ask for, it doesn't mean that He is not going to help us. Perhaps He is waiting for us to say, "Your will be done, and not mine, Lord."

Jesus asked that He be spared the agony and shame of the cross if it were possible, but He quickly added to His request, "Nevertheless, Your will be done and not Mine" (see Matthew 26:42).

We are very susceptible to asking for things that only God knows would not be good for us or will not work into His overall plan for our lives. I trust that when I ask God for help, He always says, "Yes." But I have also learned that does not necessarily mean He will help me the way I want to be helped, or that He will do it according to my timing.

God is always good—that is His very nature. Psalm 107:1

says, *"O give thanks to the Lord, for He is good; for His mercy and loving-kindness endure forever!"* We can expect God's goodness in our lives and we can look forward to it with enthusiasm and excitement. God is looking and longing for someone who's waiting for Him to be good to them. God *wants* to be good to you, but you have to be expecting Him to move in your life. Today is your day to start believing that something good is going to happen to you, and the moment you do, you will improve your day! God is working in your life right now, and He wants you to enjoy the life He has given you.

Things to remember:

- Negative and unhealthy expectations can be detrimental in our lives.
- Regardless of the pain you've been through in the past, refuse the temptation to live in dread. Don't expect the worst; hope for the best.
- We can build strong, healthy relationships with others, but we should not look to them as our source. God is our Source!
- When you need to improve your day, reexamine your expectations.

Suggestions for Putting "Reexamine Your Expectations" into Practice

- Make a list of what you are expecting and whom you are expecting it from. Make sure you are expecting good things from the right source.
- Each time you feel worry or dread over something that might go wrong, stop and thank God for His goodness and tell Him you can't wait to see what goes right today.
- When someone does something nice for you, or even if they compliment you, thank them, but remember the true source was God, and He simply chose to work through a person.

CHAPTER 5

Don't Give In to Dread

The Lord is my Light and my Salvation—whom shall I fear or dread? The Lord is the Refuge and Stronghold of my life—of whom shall I be afraid?

Psalm 27:1

Preventive action is sometimes the best and healthiest action we can take. If you can stop a problem before it gets started, your day is so much better. For example:

- When you get the oil in your car changed every three thousand miles, your car will run smoother and many engine problems can be avoided.
- When you get regular physicals, eye exams, and dental cleanings, major health problems can be prevented or detected early.
- When you spend regular time with your spouse (like date nights), your relationship will be strengthened and spared big problems down the road.

This is true not only with your car, your health, or your relationships—preventive maintenance is a crucial element in every part of your life. If you want to be healthy and at peace in your soul, it's important to stop problems before they become "strongholds" in your life. And one way you do that is when you decide, *I'm not going to give in to dread.*

Dread is the precursor to fear. It's subtle at first. Thoughts like, *Ugh, I dread this week. I have so many things to do that I don't enjoy, and my boss is back in town and the office is always more tense when he is around*—create feelings of dread that lead to a frustrated, fearful, and unhappy life.

When dread creeps in, that's when you can practice preventive maintenance. You can deal with the issue before it becomes full-blown fear or worry. You don't have to let it drain your joy. You can say, "I'm not going to dread today. I'm not going to live with that worry. I'm not going to allow this to develop into fear in my life!" Like changing your oil every three thousand miles or going for an annual checkup, dealing with dread in the early stages will help you avoid problems down the road.

What Is Dread?

Dread is nothing more than expecting something bad or unpleasant to happen. It is planning not to enjoy something you need to do. Here is why that is dangerous: It's the very opposite of hope and faith. Hope is a confident expectation of good, and faith always trusts God for the best. Faith is what God tells us to live by. We are to do all things in faith! We are to live with a positive expectation of joy and enjoyment, not an energy-draining dread.

> *We are to live with a positive expectation of joy and enjoyment, not an energy-draining dread.*

You may have thought that dreading the day ahead, being exasperated at the thought of going to work, or feeling frustrated that you have to run several errands after work is normal, but

God has so much more in store for you than living a life charac-
terized by these dreads and frustrations. 2 Timothy 1:7 says:

> For God did not give us a spirit of timidity (of cowardice,
> of craven and cringing and fawning fear), but [He has
> given us a spirit] of power and of love and of calm and
> well-balanced mind and discipline and self-control.

And Psalm 23:4 says it this way:

> Yes, though I walk through the [deep, sunless] valley
> of the shadow of death, I will fear or dread no evil, for
> You are with me; Your rod [to protect] and Your staff [to
> guide], they comfort me.

With God on your side, there is nothing you cannot overcome…
and that includes dread. So the next time you have those feelings of
dread about the day ahead, deal with them immediately. Don't allow
that foothold to become a stronghold in your life. God didn't create
you to live with a bad feeling about your day or your life. He created
you to live in the joy that comes with hope and faith for better things!

How to Stop Dread Right Away

As you read this chapter, you may be thinking, *Well, dread sounds
like something everyone faces. If that is the case, how do I stop it?
How can I live a life free from dread?*

I believe the first step toward a dread-free life is asking the Holy
Spirit to make you aware of it anytime you begin to dread something. It is not that difficult to stop dreading if you realize you are
doing it and that it is a problem, rather than merely something we

all do. When I catch myself dreading something, I say to myself, *I am not only not going to dread this, I am going to enjoy it, because God is with me in all that I do.*

The very moment you begin to feel a sense of reluctance or dread, recognize that this feeling is not from God. Whether you're dreading a household chore, a meeting with a colleague, or an upcoming trip—there is no dread that is healthy or productive in your life.

If you recognize dread at its outset, you will be able to deal with it immediately. Too many people go through life not realizing or recognizing the things that are stealing their joy. They have miserable days... but they don't even know why. If you see dread for what it is—a joy-stealer—you'll be able to fight it right away. That brings me to...

Take It to God

Too many times we try to fight battles in our own strength and then, when we inevitably fail, we get frustrated and want to give up. I suggest that anytime you recognize you are feeling dread about the day ahead—take it to God. Tell Him, "Father, I'm feeling a sense of unease and dread about (this or that). If it is something You don't want me to do, please show me, and if You do want me to do it, then grant me grace to do it with joy." Anytime we take our problems to God, we are in a better position to enjoy our day. God can do things through us that we could never do on our own,

> God can do things through us that we could never do on our own, so don't try to battle dread alone.

so don't try to battle dread alone. If we focus on enjoying God and His companionship, it can make an unpleasant task something we can do with a good attitude.

Find the Good in Everything

I've discovered there is great strength in speaking positive, faith-filled words over my day. Rather than talking about all the things I'm dreading, when I speak God's promises over the day to come, incredible things happen.

Instead of saying, "Oh, I can't believe I have to go grocery shopping today; it's going to be a madhouse in there," say something like, "I'm so grateful I have money for groceries, and a car to get me to the store."

Instead of saying, "Ugh, it looks like rain today. The weather is going to be miserable and my hair is going to be a mess. How depressing," say something like, "Rain or shine, I'm going to have a good day. Something as simple as the weather is not going to dictate my happiness!"

Instead of saying, "I have so much work to do this week. I'm dreading it all. I can't wait until this week is over," say something like, "It looks like a challenging week ahead, but I can't wait to see what God is going to do. I'm going to do my best and then trust Him to do the rest. I'm excited to see how it will all turn out!"

Do you see the difference? When you change the conversation, you stop dread dead in its tracks. Don't speak words that can actually create problems; have the faith to speak about God's promises, because that opens the door for Him to work in your life.

Put Your Hope in God's Word

I believe the Word of God is the very best solution for dread, fear, and worry. If you dedicate yourself to study the Word, learning the promises of God

> *The Word of God is the very best solution for dread, fear, and worry.*

for your life, there is no way you will wilt under the pressure of dread. When dread tries to ruin your day, you'll be able to overcome it with the truth of God's Word.

I think about many of the examples in the Word of God—Peter, David, Ruth, Esther, Mary, Abraham, Moses. All of these heroes of faith went through difficult days. They all could have given in to dread and fear, but rather than shrink back when challenges arose, they chose to trust God and move forward. What great examples for you and for me! If we will spend time studying God's promises and drawing strength from these examples (and so many others), there is no way dread can win. God's Word is His primary way of speaking to us. If we cherish it, we'll overcome dread every time. I would never have even known that dread was a problem in my life had I not found it out by studying God's Word! Satan used dread to drain my joy and energy for many years, but God's Word taught me that I could resist it and put a stop to it in my life, and so can you.

Dare to Be Defiant

When it comes to dread, I want to encourage you to be determined…to be diligent…to be defiant. Part of the definition of the word "defiant" is to be uncooperative. It is time for us to stop cooperating with dread! Make it your mission to eradicate dread at every turn. Recognize that nothing good can ever come from dread and decide to reject it whenever it tries to show up in your life.

It's easy to assume that because something is challenging, there is no way you can enjoy it, but with God's help you can do amazing things. You can even learn to enjoy doing things that you once dreaded! When we expect that the worst is going to happen, it only leads to a frustrated, miserable, unhappy life. Why not choose something better? Choose hope and faith and allow God to surprise you with His goodness. It doesn't matter what you have to do in the days to come, God can turn it into something enjoyable.

Even the most menial tasks can be done with joy. With the right attitude, doing dishes can be a time of reflecting on the goodness of God. Cleaning house can become a time to pray for others. With a different mind-set, the long commute can be a time when you get some work done that you need to do. With the proper perspective, the *obstacle* at work can be turned into the *opportunity* at work. It's all about being defiant enough to say no to dread and yes to hope and faith. Make that choice today and you'll find that you'll enjoy today much more than you ever thought possible. You can make any day more enjoyable by refusing to dread anything you need to do!

Things to remember:

- Dread is the precursor to fear. When dread creeps in, that's when you can practice preventive maintenance. You can deal with the issue before it becomes full-blown fear and worry.
- Dread is the very opposite of hope and faith.
- The very moment you begin to feel a sense of reluctance or dread, recognize that that feeling is not from God.
- When you speak God's promises over the day to come, instead of talking about all the things you're dreading, incredible things happen.

Suggestions for Putting "Don't Give In to Dread" into Practice

- Turn a feeling of dread into a feeling of hope. The next time you're dreading something, think the opposite, hoping for God to do the very best.
- Think of three positive, hope-filled thoughts you can have right now about the day ahead.
- Defy dread and refuse to let it poison your day.

SECTION II

New Steps to Take

The steps of a [good] man are directed and established by the Lord.

Psalm 37:23

CHAPTER 6

Learn Something New

A mind that is stretched by a new experience can never go back to its old dimensions.

—Oliver Wendell Holmes

When was the last time you tried to learn something new? A new fact about history? The definition of a new word? A new hobby? A new job skill? Made a new friend? I think that learning new things adds interest and pleasure to any day.

I ask this question because too many people (including Christians) are living stale, stagnant lives simply because they've stopped learning. They're not exercising curiosity, broadening their horizons, or testing their limits—they're not doing anything new. Each day looks like the last: same routine, same mind-set, same activities, and maybe even the same misery.

If you can relate to the boredom of "same," I've got good news for you: You don't have to stay stuck in the *same* routines, dealing with the *same* frustrations day in and day out. One of the easiest (and most enjoyable) things you can do to enjoy your life is make the decision to start learning new, exciting, different things. It doesn't have to be something big or complicated; it may be something as simple as learning a new exercise routine, how to plant a garden, or how to do more with your computer than

> *If you'll dedicate yourself to learning on a regular (if not daily) basis, you'll be amazed at how much fun you'll have in the discovery of new things.*

just send emails. It's different for each person, but if you'll dedicate yourself to learning on a regular (if not daily) basis, you'll be amazed at how much fun you'll have in the discovery of new things.

One of the ways I choose to learn new things is by watching documentaries. There are endless stories about amazing people who have done amazing things, or people who have been through very tragic things and have made the decision to not let it make them bitter. You can find documentaries about famous people, places you have never been, the animal kingdom, nature, and so on. These stories are not only interesting, they are inspiring.

Learning is often a process of trial and error. Don't get discouraged if you try something and find it isn't right for you. Try something else and keep trying until you find a way to learn on a regular basis. Learning isn't as easy for some as it is for others. We are not all as quick at learning as Hoagy Carmichael...

A story is told about the composer and bandleader Howard Hoagland "Hoagy" Carmichael and his decision to take up golf. Interested in the sport, Carmichael scheduled lessons with a golf instructor and showed up on the assigned day ready to learn.

At the first lesson, Carmichael listened patiently as the instructor showed him the basics of the game: things like how to hold a golf club, how to stand over the ball, the mechanics of a golf swing, and so on. About a half hour into this first lesson, the instructor said, "Why don't you get out the driver and try to hit the ball in the direction of the first hole." Carmichael teed up the golf ball and swung the club as hard as he could. He watched it fly down the fairway, bounce onto the green, and roll directly into the cup—a hole in one!

The instructor couldn't believe what he had just seen. He was speechless. Without missing a beat, Carmichael turned to the dumbfounded instructor and said with a twinkle in his eye, "Ok, I think I've got the idea now."[3]

As I said, we can't all "learn" as quickly as Hoagy Carmichael, but we can all learn. We can learn new skills, we can learn new parenting techniques, we can learn new styles and trends, we can learn a new profession—the options are endless. There is so much more we can learn and there are so many ways that new knowledge can increase our joy and improve our lives. I see countless people with headphones plugged into their ears while they walk, exercise, clean their house, and many other things. Times like those are great opportunities to learn. If you are a person who loves to listen to music during such times, that is great, because music can be very inspiring, but perhaps you could consider taking just thirty minutes of the time to learn something new!

I have discovered I can listen to at least thirty minutes of some kind of Bible teaching just during the time it takes me to put on makeup and fix my hair each morning. If you think you don't have time to learn new things, you may be surprised by what you can accomplish. All you need to do is take advantage of the opportunities that are right in front of you. Start using the power of the half hour! It is amazing what we can accomplish if we use fifteen minutes here and there, or the thirty minutes that are available between appointments. These are times we often waste and that we could use in a more productive way.

Don't be deceived by thinking that you must have a long time to read or listen to learn something. Use some of the shorter spurts of time you have and they will add up to a lot of time invested instead of wasted.

Learn More About God

The more we learn about God, the closer we can be to Him. The Apostle Paul said that his determined purpose in life was to know Jesus and the power of His resurrection (see Philippians 3:10). The Amplified Bible uses terminology to explain the deep meaning of this verse that I want to share with you, and I ask that you take time to really think about what it is saying:

> [For my determined purpose is] that I may know Him [that I may progressively become more deeply and intimately acquainted with Him, perceiving and recognizing and understanding the wonders of His Person more strongly and more clearly], and that I may in that same way come to know the power outflowing from His resurrection [which it exerts over believers], and that I may so share His sufferings as to be continually transformed [in spirit into His likeness].
>
> Philippians 3:10

This one verse of Scripture is so powerful that we should never tire of pondering it, hoping to understand it better. All too often we are guilty of seeking God only for help with our problems, and when we live this way, we rob ourselves of the beauty and power of learning how absolutely wonderful He is in countless ways; we miss the opportunity to develop a closer and more intimate relationship with Him.

If you are interested in learning more about God, let me recommend a thorough study on the character of God. I have a series of teachings on this subject, and there are many great books available on the subject by several different authors. When you know

God's character, it helps you trust Him more and more. When we trust Him, we can enter His rest and give up worrying and being afraid.

Of course there are countless things that I can suggest that you learn about God, but instead of getting into specific subjects, let me share with you how learning more about God has impacted my life, and it can do the same for you.

Jesus said that when we study His Word, we are transformed, or entirely changed into His image, and I can say that He has changed me! The more we learn about Him, the more we become like Him, and that should be the goal of every child of God. His love is unfathomable. It is beyond anything we can understand with our finite minds, but the more I have learned about Him, the more I have become convinced that He does indeed love me, and I know that He loves you also. As you learn how much He loves you, it will enable you to accept yourself and have confidence to live your life fully. It will also help you to experience the joy of truly loving other people.

This book is about ways to make every day better, and I can honestly say that I rarely have a day now when I think, *I'm just having a bad day!* But before I started truly *learning* about God in a deeper and more intimate way, most of my days were bad days. Yes, I was a Christian, but I did not know God. I knew about Him, but that is not enough. We need to know Him and the power of His resurrection and the wonders of His Person!

The ways that are available to us today to learn more about God are too many to accurately count. You can choose many simple methods of learning more and easily fit them into your day. For example, keep devotionals in a few different places in your home and as time is available, read one or more of the devotions and either learn something new or remind yourself of something you have learned in the past. Keep one in your car, at your office, in your briefcase, and other places where you might have a few minutes to read, and then do it!

Learn More About Yourself

Have you ever thought of taking time to truly learn about yourself? You are quite amazing, but you may not know it. Use the Internet, or get a book and learn about how the human body functions and what God has created it to do. For example, you have six quarts of blood in your body, and it circulates through your body three times each minute. That means that your blood travels twelve thousand miles each day inside your body in order to keep you healthy!

Your heart beats 35 million times each year! You have 60,000 blood vessels inside your body. Nerve impulses travel to the brain at a speed of 250 miles per hour. And these are just a few things about you that make you so amazing, and clearly show how amazing our Creator is!

Did you know that you are unique and that there is no one on earth who is exactly like you...and God fashioned you very carefully with His own hands in your mother's womb? (See Psalm 139.)

Get to know your strengths and weaknesses. What you truly enjoy and the kind of work you are suited for. What are your limitations? Do you enjoy spending time alone, and if not, why not? You are such a great person, and you should take time to get to know yourself better. Another thing you need to learn how to do is to totally accept and love yourself. It is impossible to enjoy this day or any other day if you don't love yourself! You don't have to love everything you do, but you do need to love the basic person God created when He made you. Decide to enjoy yourself today and every day! Learn to laugh at yourself more!

A study of the different personality types is eye-opening. If you have never done it, you will thoroughly enjoy it and it will help you learn more about yourself, as well as the other people in your life.

The Internet is loaded with information of all kinds. You can learn something and not even have to work at it very hard. You can get information in segments as short as two or three minutes, or find a seminar that's several hours long. Thankfully, libraries and stores where books are sold are filled with books. In addition, we have CDs, DVDs, podcasts, YouTube videos, digital downloads of messages and books, and it is possible that by the time this book reaches your hands, several more methods of learning will have been created. I think it is safe to say that anyone who wants to learn has more tools available than at any other time in history.

The only thing left for you to do is begin! I am sure you are learning things, but hopefully this chapter will help you realize that you can learn even more and that it will not only make your day seem more alive and exciting, but if you keep it up long enough, your entire life may become that way!

Things to remember:

- Many people (including Christians) are living stale, stagnant lives simply because they've stopped learning.
- Learning is often a process of trial and error. Don't get discouraged if you try to learn a new skill or hobby and it doesn't work out right away.
- The best thing you can learn is more about God and His incredible, never-ending love for you.
- You can use small amounts of time and they will add up to lots of beneficial learning.

Suggestions for Putting "Learn Something New" into Practice

- Make a list of things that you would like to learn about, and start learning.
- Try to learn one amazing fact about how your body functions each day.
- If you don't use a computer, go buy a book on amazing facts and learn some things you never knew before.
- If you cook, learn how to make something you have never made before.

CHAPTER 7

Refuse to Settle

Excellence is doing ordinary things extraordinarily well.
—John W. Garner

Let's do a little exercise together. It's going to require some imagination on your part. We'll call it "The 'What If' Story":

What if you grew up in approximately the center of the United States . . . let's say in Wichita, Kansas. And what if your dream was to live by the ocean. You've vacationed on the East Coast numerous times, and you absolutely love the salt air, the sand under your feet, and fresh seafood for dinner every night. Some people like the plains, some people like the mountains, but you? You like the beach . . . actually, you love it!

And what if you decided, *I'm going for it! I'm going to sell my house, pack up the moving truck, and I'm following my dream. Atlantic Ocean, here I come!* Good for you! How exciting! You're going on an adventure. You're going to have such a great story to tell, and you're going to *love* telling it from the comfort of your beach chair!

You make the necessary arrangements. Your friends all come over and help you pack. You say goodbye to Wichita, start up your overstuffed moving truck, and pull out onto the highway, heading east. You can almost smell the salt air already!

But what if you start getting tired after driving for a few hours?

And what if you begin to dread how much farther you still have to go? And what if you begin to think about how much you enjoyed living in Kansas all those years? Your excitement starts to wane, and your resolve starts to weaken. You are sure you will miss all of your friends. Maybe the beach isn't such a great place after all. I mean, come on, it's going to take a long time to get there!

And what if... just six or seven hours into your drive... you come upon the mighty Mississippi River? *Hmm*, you think, *I could live a pretty nice life here.* Sure, it's not the ocean, but it's still water. Okay, it's not the beach, but it still has sand. Obviously, it doesn't have seafood, but it still has fish. It might not be your dream, but it's still pretty nice.

And what if you pull the truck over, think about it for a moment, and decide, *This isn't such a bad place. I'll just settle here.*

Now, if you live in Wichita, or anywhere along the Mississippi River, don't get upset with me—they are lovely places to live. (I know, because I live in St. Louis, Missouri, and the Mississippi runs right through it.) I'm just using these places as examples. Wherever you call home, I want you to engage in this "what if" exercise because there is an important life lesson I want you to understand: *Anytime you set out for the ocean but settle for a river, you're missing out.*

> Anytime we settle (or compromise) for something less than our destination, it costs us something.

I've seen this truth revealed time and time again in my own life and in the lives of others. Anytime we settle (or compromise) for something less than our destination, it costs us something:

- If we set out to love people but settle for tolerating them, we miss out on deep and lasting relationships.

- If we set out to study the Word of God but settle for reading it every once in a while, when it's convenient for us, we miss out on having a solid foundation for our lives.
- If we set out to be the best employee we can be but settle for being a good employee when the boss is around, we miss out on the satisfaction of a job well done.
- If we set out to complete a project with excellence but settle for just getting the project done with as little effort as possible, we miss out on the reward and the recognition that comes along with a spirit of excellence.

Mediocrity is the midway point between two destinations. It always caves when there is a conflict and pauses when there is a problem. Mediocrity is easy—anybody can do it—but it's costly. It costs us accomplishment. It costs us fulfillment. And it costs us real joy. It is entirely possible that you could make

> *Mediocrity is easy—anybody can do it—but it's costly.*

your day better by refusing mediocrity and making a decision to be excellent in all you do today and every day.

It's only when you refuse to settle for mediocre that you'll really begin to enjoy every day and experience the overcoming, abundant life Jesus came to give you.

Are You in Canaan or Haran?

I remember when I first saw this principle—refusing to settle for mediocrity—in the Word of God. It's an obscure passage, and you'll miss it if you're not looking carefully (another reason why studying the Word of God, not just reading it, is so important), but it is certainly there for us to learn from.

Genesis 11 is a chapter filled mostly with genealogies. You know, So-and-so became the father of Such-and-such. Admittedly, genealogies aren't always the most exciting chapters in the Bible, and we are sometimes tempted to skip right past them. But that would be a mistake. There is a lot to glean from these passages of Scripture. Genesis 11:31 is a perfect example.

We have all heard about Abraham, but in Genesis 11:31 we get a rare glimpse into the life of his father, Terah. Terah had three sons—Abraham, Nahor, and Haran. And in Genesis 11:31, this is what we learn about Terah:

> And Terah took Abram his son, Lot the son of Haran, his grandson, and Sarai his daughter-in-law, his son Abram's wife, and they went forth together to go from Ur of the Chaldees into the land of Canaan; but when they came to Haran, **they settled there.**

Did you see it? Terah set out for Canaan but he *settled* in Haran. This is just like our "what if" exercise. Canaan was his destination, but Haran was his compromise.

I wonder how many people have a destination but settle for less. Whether it's in their job, their relationships, the way they take care of themselves, their walk with God—how many times do they have a goal but settle for far less than God's best?

Let me make this more personal: How many times have you settled for mediocrity? How many times have you set out for Canaan but settled in Haran? Are you obeying God in *some*

> *How many times have you set out for Canaan but settled in Haran?*

things rather than in everything? Are you forgiving *some* offenses rather than all of them? Are you giving God control of *part* of your life but not all of it? Are you asking God to fix *other* people without asking Him to do His work in your life?

All of these things are pictures of mediocrity. They are a midpoint between two destinations. Your intention is good (you want to get to the ocean), but your determination is lacking (you've settled for a river). Rather than reaching for excellence, you've rested in mediocrity. And anytime you do that, frustration is soon to follow. If you really want to take an important step to enjoying each new day, let me ask you to consider again...

What If?

Going back to our original illustration, let's look at "what if" in a different way: What if you had kept driving to the beach even when you were tired of the road? What if you had resisted the temptation to look back, choosing only to look forward? What if you had refused to settle for a river when the ocean was your dream?

The answers are simple. You would have lived out your dream—salt water, white sand, fresh fish for dinner! Had you been determined enough to push for excellence, rather than settling for less, you would have experienced the joys of your destination. With that in mind, let me take this from an illustration and bring it into real life:

- What if you gave God your all?
- What if you confronted problems instead of running from them?
- What if you demanded the best from yourself instead of "average"?
- What if you did today what you could put off until tomorrow?

- What if you held fast to your integrity by always keeping your word?
- What if you chose to be excellent when the world around you is mediocre?

I don't know where you are in your life or in your walk with God right now, but I do know this: If you refuse to settle for mediocre, you'll be well on your way to experiencing God's best. If you don't, then you are headed for disappointment, dissatisfaction, and a lack of fulfillment. In your relationships, in your health, in your family, in your career, and in your faith—God has more in store than you can imagine. Keep driving...the beach will be here before you know it!

Things to remember:

- Anytime you compromise and stop short of your destination, you're missing out.
- Abraham's father, Terah, was traveling to Canaan, but he "settled" in Haran. How many times have you settled for Haran when Canaan was just around the corner?
- Mediocrity is simply the midpoint between two destinations.
- Problems and difficulties tempt us to give up. If you push past the obstacles, you'll experience God's best for your life.

Suggestions for Putting "Refuse to Settle" into Practice

- Rather than complain about mediocrity in others, look for it in your own life. Are there areas where you have "settled"?
- Find something in your schedule that is not bearing good fruit and give it up, in order to give more time and energy to something else that is truly important to you.
- If there are areas in your life where you feel like you have settled for less than the best, don't get under condemnation. Instead, be proactive. Think of some ways to improve the situation and begin to put those into place.
- Look at the tasks before you today. Choose to do each of them with excellence and then do it!

CHAPTER 8

Invest in Yourself

Your success depends mainly on what you think of yourself and whether you believe in yourself.

—William J. H. Boetcker

When we hear the words "invest" or "investing" our minds naturally go to finance. We might picture *investment bankers* in nice suits shouting out numbers on the floor of the New York Stock Exchange. Or we may think of an entrepreneur in the family who presented us with an *investment opportunity* where we could "get in on the ground floor." Investing hits close to home for many people who *invest* part of their paychecks on a regular basis in order to prepare for retirement.

I'm not an economist or a financial consultant, but the concept for investing is pretty simple: The more you invest, the longer you invest, and the better you invest, the better the return on your investment. Another way to say it is this: The more you put in now, you'll get that and so much more back later. The benefits of wise investing are numerous—financial security, college tuition for your kids or grandkids, a comfortable retirement, the chance to do new things, like travel, and (Dave's favorite) golf, golf, golf! It's not easy—investing requires discipline and sacrifice—but it pays off in the end.

As important as all of that is, I believe there is a type of investment that is even more important than financial investment. And that investment is taking the daily opportunity to invest in yourself. Your health, your peace of mind, your personal growth, your joy and happiness—these are all things impacted by how little or how much you choose to invest in your own life.

And much like financial investing, the more you invest in yourself, the longer you invest in yourself, and the better you invest in yourself all determine what kind of return you are going to get on your investment. If you'll be disciplined now to invest properly in your health and well-being, the physical, emotional, and spiritual benefits will come pouring in.

> *The more you invest in yourself, the longer you invest in yourself, and the better you invest in yourself all determine what kind of return you are going to get on your investment.*

That's why "Invest in Yourself" is one of the best ways you can make every day better. It helps you today... but it also helps you in the days, weeks, months, and years to come!

I want to give you some very specific ways to invest in yourself, but first let me ask this question:

Why Don't We Take Better Care of Ourselves?

It's really pretty perplexing. If we recognize the importance of investing financially, why don't we invest in the rest of our lives—physically, emotionally, and spiritually? I meet so many people who are not taking care of themselves (and for many years I was one of them). They're going through life weak, exhausted, and discouraged, just trying to keep their heads above water.

Their lives would be so much better if they would simply invest in themselves. Let me share with you a few reasons why people (maybe even you) neglect to properly take care of themselves.

1. We may feel that we are being selfish if we spend time and money on ourselves. But the truth is that if we don't take care of ourselves, eventually we won't have anything to give to anyone else. The best gift you can give to your family and friends is a healthy you.

2. We don't have the proper information. For many years, we've been inundated with prepackaged, processed food, fast foods, fad diets, no information, or misinformation. All of this has left us with a lot of confusion about what is really healthy and what isn't. And it's not just food—for years we've been sold shallow self-help books and questionable "instant success" schemes that prey upon our desire for quick fixes and require no effort on our part. What we really need is proper information that gives us *real* answers for our physical, emotional, and spiritual needs.

3. We've become too busy to exercise. Until recently, exercise was something we got plenty of during the course of an ordinary day. People walked a lot, worked hard, and sweated the toxins out of their bodies. But today, if we are going to get any exercise, many of us have to book it into our schedules and do it purposely. The problem is we are busy with other things that instead of investing in our bodies, we fill up the calendar with other activities, many of which are stressful and actually zap the energy we do have. Our calendars are getting bigger and bigger while our bodies are getting weaker and weaker.

4. We've allowed advertising and media to damage our body image. In order to sell their products, advertisers give us mixed messages. On one hand, they inundate us with messages of dangerous, unattainable images of what beauty should look like in order to sell their skincare products, clothing, and other accessories. At the same time, the makers of unhealthy, prepackaged food spend advertising dollars so we'll buy their products. With all of this conflicting information, many people don't know what to think about body image. We need to reset our internal picture of what a healthy person should look like, and not be so quick to believe every ad we see.

5. **We've allowed our lives to become too fast-paced.** Because of the incredible pressures of juggling career and parenthood, paying steep mortgages and inflated bills, and burning the proverbial candle at both ends on most days, it is very difficult to invest in healthy living. It's much easier to put off the workout and grab a cheeseburger on the run. It's a daily temptation to sleep less in order to catch up on paperwork or something else work-related. The sad thing is that we are letting our busy schedule squeeze out everything that once gave us pleasure. Life is a gift and is meant to be joyful—we should slow down and enjoy that gift.

6. **We're trying to do it alone.** When we don't have a good support system or godly foundation to keep our spirits high, it becomes easy to slip into bad habits rooted in loneliness and discouragement. We need to spend regular time in fellowship with God, asking Him to give us wisdom to live a healthy life, and remember that we don't have to go someplace special to talk to God, because He is everywhere all the time and is always excited to hear from us. We also need to have the right people around us, who will encourage us and speak up if they see us getting out of balance. Great friendships and compassionate support can be the difference between healthy and unhealthy living.

7. **We have forgotten our own value.** I believe this is the biggest reason we neglect to take care of ourselves. If you don't

understand how important you are to God, taking care of yourself seems pointless. Reminding yourself of your value and your place in God's plan is very important. You are with you all the time, and if you don't value yourself, you're not likely to enjoy the day.

Learning to Value Yourself in Order to Invest in Yourself

We all understand that we have relationships with other people, but did it ever occur to you that you have a relationship with yourself? Think about it: You spend more time with yourself than anyone else. You are the person you can never get away from. At some time in your life, you probably went to school with another student or worked with someone whom you didn't really get along with. That can be frustrating, but at least they didn't come home with you each night. You can't get away from yourself, not even for one second, so it's very important that you have peace with yourself and value the person God created you to be.

It doesn't matter what society or the culture says about your worth—the only thing that matters is what God says! The widely respected Danish theologian Søren Kierkegaard once told a parable about two thieves who broke into a jewelry store. Instead of stealing the jewelry, they simply switched all the price tags. They put the high-priced tags on the cheaper jewelry and the low-priced tags on the most valuable gems. And for several weeks not a single person noticed. People paid outrageous prices for the cheaper jewelry and rock-bottom prices for the finest jewels. Kierkegaard's point was pretty obvious: We live in a world where someone has switched the price tags.

- The world may label you as worthless, but God labels you as His masterpiece (see Ephesians 2:10).

- The world may label you as an accident, but God labels you as fearfully and wonderfully made (see Psalm 139:14).
- The world may label you as rejected, but God labels you as chosen (see Colossians 3:12) and deeply loved (see Jeremiah 31:3).

When you feel worthless, rejected, inferior, or insignificant, all you have to do is switch the price tags. That label may be what someone said about you or how society makes you feel about yourself, but it's not what God says. And God's opinion is the only thing that matters. You're significant, you're valuable, and you're worth the investment, because God says you are!

You're significant, you're valuable, and you're worth the investment, because God says you are!

We must come to a place where we value ourselves, not out of pride or arrogance, but out of confidence in who we are in Christ. We should be able to say, "I know God loves me, so I can love and value what God chooses to love and value. I don't love everything I do, but I accept myself because God accepts me." We can learn to become spiritually mature enough to understand that even when God shows us a change that is needed in us, He is doing it because He loves us and wants the best for us. We can say, "I believe God is changing me daily, but during this process, I will not devalue what God values. I'll accept myself because God accepts me. Jesus sees what I am right now, but He also sees what I am becoming, and He loves me in every stage of my growth and maturity as His child."

As you begin to see yourself as God sees you—someone who's valued and cherished—your view of yourself will begin to change. You'll see yourself as a person who is worth investing in.

How to Invest in Yourself

Now that you know that you're valuable and worth investing in, let me give you some specific ways you can do that. These may be things you've never thought of, or they may just be reminders of things you know are important. Either way, let this list serve as motivation to start investing in yourself—spirit, soul, *and* body.

You can start investing in yourself today by:

- Deciding to get some daily exercise. Walking, jogging, swimming, lifting weights, playing sports with the kids—however you choose to exercise, make a plan and stick to it.
- Getting the proper amount of sleep. If you can't wake up any later because of morning responsibilities, be disciplined enough to go to bed earlier. A proper amount of rest is crucial in taking care of your body.
- Nurturing and developing your mind. Read books, be creative, increase your vocabulary, keep your brain active. Find ways to stimulate your mind and increase your learning.
- Eliminating destructive, unhealthy habits. No more excuses—today can be the day you finally quit that habit that is ruining your health and stealing your peace.
- Beginning a new, healthy habit. The best way to quit a bad habit is to start a good habit! What is something that you find interesting that could be a new healthy part of your life? Laughing more, gardening, walking your dog, eating more organic food—get creative!
- Changing your diet. There is so much information available these days about the nutritional value of the food you're eating. This wasn't always the case, but thankfully, we're getting better and better information about our food and

various nutritional options. If we want to feel and look better, it's essential that we are educated in what we need to eat, and that we are aware of what we are eating.

- Pursuing your skills and developing your talents. Find the things that you are naturally good at, spend time practicing them, and get even better. If you put time and effort into developing the skills God has given you, you'll be surprised at the doors of opportunity that will open for you.

- No longer doing things that steal your time and destroy your joy. We don't always get to do everything we want to do; we all have duties and obligations that require our attention. However, many times we allow unnecessary things to steal our time. If there is something that is causing you pressure and wasting your time, get rid of it. Life is too short to waste it on things that are unproductive and stressful. Find out what you truly love doing, and make sure to put time into your schedule to do it.

- Building your confidence. I've found that a confident person is a happier person. Study what God has to say about you. Surround yourself with people who will encourage and inspire you. Focus on your strengths, not your weaknesses. These are all keys to confidence.

These are just a few of the many, many ways you can invest in yourself. As you read these, you may have even come up with a few more ideas of your own. Whatever you choose to do, remember that investment takes discipline and even some sacrifice. It's not always easy at first and it may take time to develop these new, healthy habits, but there is one thing you can be sure about: A good investment in yourself always pays off in the long run. God wants you to invest in you!

Things to remember:

- Make an investment in yourself!
- We often fail to take care of ourselves because we don't see ourselves the way that God sees us.
- Don't allow a busy, fast pace of life keep you from taking the time needed to exercise, rest, and eat properly.
- Accepting yourself and seeing value in yourself is not prideful or arrogant; it's simply realizing that you are a child of God. Because He values you, you should value yourself.
- Investing in yourself will take discipline and sacrifice, but it is worth it in the long run.

Suggestions for Putting "Invest in Yourself" into Practice

- Take out a record-keeping ledger and use it to evaluate your daily routine. Look at how many things in today's ledger are deposits in your life, as opposed to how many things are withdrawals.
- Draw up some "price tags." Instead of what the world says about you, write on the price tags some of the things God says about you and what He loves about you.
- Tell your spouse or a friend one thing you are going to do today to invest in yourself. Ask them to call you at the end of the day to see if you were able to follow through. Knowing that phone call is coming will serve as extra incentive.

CHAPTER 9

Be Adventurous

Life is either a great adventure or nothing at all.
—Helen Keller

Can you think of an event or a season in your life that was all about adventure? Maybe it was when you were a kid and traveled with your parents on an exciting family vacation. Or maybe it was the exhilaration of going off to college. Perhaps you look back fondly on the first years of marriage when everything seemed fresh and new. Adventure comes in many forms. You don't have to be a daredevil or a thrill seeker to be adventurous. You can have adventures in your career, with your family, in your downtime, and even in your relationship with God. I know that has certainly been true in my life.

Do you remember those vintage bubble trailers from the 1950s? You don't see them around much anymore, but they used to be pretty popular on America's highways. They were great for storing stuff, they weren't too heavy to haul, and they looked like...well, they looked like *bubbles*. Every time Dave and I see one of these trailers, it reminds us of a season of adventure in our ministry and in our marriage. You see, in the early days of our ministry, a bubble trailer was how we carted our ministry equipment around with us. Our ministry team wasn't nearly as large as it is now. In the early days, it was just me and Dave, and a guy who could sing and play guitar.

I still remember that even though it was difficult, we were so excited just to be ministering the Word of God. Our meetings were pretty small in those days. We didn't travel very far—just to different churches and venues in and around St. Louis. We didn't know for sure what God was doing behind the scenes, but we had big dreams for the future. They were days mixed with fear and excitement, days of meager finances, lots of hard work, disappointments and thrills, but here we are today, and things have certainly changed since those early days.

By the grace of God, we are able to teach the Word and share the love of Christ with people all around the world. We've seen thousands saved at crusades, countless children in third-world countries fed and cared for, our television program broadcast in countries on every continent, and millions ministered to by our various missions initiatives. And I will admit that at times, I can lose my sense of adventure and just settle into the "work and responsibility" of it all. But when I do, I always sense a lack of enjoyment and I purpose to become adventurous again.

I believe having a sense of adventure is crucial to enjoying the life God has given you. Adventure doesn't have to be something expensive or over the top—my story proves that you can be adventurous doing something as simple as hauling a trailer. It's all about your outlook. If you view each day of your life as a big opportunity rather than a

> *If you view each day of your life as a big opportunity rather than a boring obligation, adventure comes alive!*

boring obligation, adventure comes alive! Keep in mind that you are on a journey with God, and what could be any more exciting and adventurous than that?

- You can turn a trip to the park with your kids or grandkids into a treasure hunt. *Adventure!*
- You can shake things up on date night. Rather than the same restaurant and movie theater, explore a new place to eat and a new post-dinner activity. *Adventure!*
- Your job doesn't have to be boring. You can think "outside the box," proposing a new strategy or taking initiative with a bold idea. *Adventure!*
- Rather than staying safe in your spiritual comfort zone, why not sign up to serve in a new ministry or set out on a missions trip? *Adventure!*

In order to make every day better, one of the most enjoyable steps is to make every day some sort of adventure. Being adventurous is more about our attitude than anything else. Don't be a bitter person who sits back, complaining enviously about the exciting life your friend, neighbor, or coworker is living. *Well, if I had that much money,* or *I wish I had as much spare time as they do!* Don't be jealous of others, and don't make excuses.

It's not about money or time; it's about choosing to enjoy your life…every day…no matter what. We all tend to settle into our routine, and that is not bad, but we need to mix adventure in with it, or it will become a source of misery and we may live for years without realizing what we are missing.

Choose to Be Bold and Unafraid to Fail

Throughout Scripture, God calls us to be bold—to be brave, daring, courageous, and valiant. If you have the tendency to avoid taking chances in life because you're afraid of making mistakes, God wants you to know He's pleased when you're at least bold enough to try. It doesn't matter if you don't do everything exactly right. What matters is that you step out in faith, believing God will help you!

2 Timothy 1:7 says:

> For God did not give us a spirit of timidity (of cowardice, of craven and cringing and fawning fear), **but [He has given us a spirit] of power** and of love and of calm and well-balanced mind and discipline and self-control.

God has given us "a spirit of power," and He wants us to use it! It doesn't take courage to do what we already know we can do. True courage is displayed when you're afraid to do something but you go ahead and do it anyway. The truth is, we don't ever have to give in to fear, because

True courage is displayed when you're afraid to do something but you go ahead and do it anyway.

we can ask God for His help anytime we need it.

I've noticed that many people are so afraid of making a mistake that they don't do anything. They're frozen in fear. Instead of having an adventurous spirit—instead of trying something new—they sit around wondering, *What if I'm wrong? What if I mess up? What if I don't enjoy it? What will people think?* This is just a waste of energy and a sure way to live safe, boring, less-than-God's-best lives. We're all human. We're going to make mistakes and look silly from time to time. But if we allow the fear of being judged, criticized, or laughed at to stop us, we'll never make progress in life. Sometimes I get really tired of eating the same kinds of food all the time, and I have been known to murmur about it even recently, but I hesitate to try new things because I am concerned I won't like it! I only have two choices, and they are: (1) Keep eating the same things and not enjoy it; (2) Try something new and take a chance of not enjoying it, but create a possibility of finding something new I absolutely love! It is entirely up to me which I choose.

Concerning making mistakes, what matters to God is our heart, not our performance. God knows we aren't perfect, and He's totally okay with it. The problem is, the devil knows it too, and he does his best to remind us of our imperfections as often as we'll receive it. Satan often attacks without giving notice, and when he does, we need to fight.

> The weapons we fight with are not the weapons of the world. On the contrary, they have divine power to demolish strongholds. We demolish arguments and every pretension that sets itself up against the knowledge of God, and we take captive every thought to make it obedient to Christ.
>
> 2 Corinthians 10:4–5 NIV

The devil loves to remind us of our mistakes, but just because we make a mistake doesn't mean we are a mistake! The biggest mistake we can make is to be afraid of making one.

I encourage you to stop being held hostage by the fear of making mistakes, because you will make mistakes—we all will. God is not asking you *not* to make any mistakes. He's calling you to be bold. He's calling you to be fearless in approaching life, in stepping out in faith, and in trusting Him to lead you.

Adventure and Faith Go Hand in Hand

God has great adventures for our lives. It's exciting when He puts dreams and desires in our hearts, but it can also be challenging, because adversity always comes against us when we try new things. That's why so many people fail to move forward—the road-blocks in the path ahead intimidate them. But instead of giving up at the thought of a challenge, we can choose to be bold, confident, and courageous through Christ.

God doesn't want us to live timid, shy, weak, wimpy, fearful, boring lives. He wants us to be bold, confident, and courageous, unafraid to try new things. And it never ceases to amaze me what God will do through a person who simply steps out in faith.

> *It never ceases to amaze me what God will do through a person who simply steps out in faith.*

When God asks you to leave the familiar behind—to set out on any new adventure—let His Word encourage you to keep moving forward. Because when you step into what God has for you, His anointing makes the impossible possible. 1 John 2:27 says, *"But as for you, the anointing (the sacred appointment, the unction) which you received from Him abides [permanently] in you."* I want you to let that sink in: God's anointing (His presence and power) abides permanently in you. So why should you live a boring life when there's a great, adventurous life available to you?

Instead of becoming timid and doubtful when we face the new challenges adventure brings, we can learn to face those challenges head-on. I have to apply this same principle to my life all the time. Let me share one example with you:

Years ago, we realized that we really needed more office space. At the same time, we needed more employees, which would require more desks, computers, phones, and so on. *We had a choice.* We had prayed for growth so we could help more people, and everything did increase—resource orders, speaking engagements, incoming phone calls, mail. It was God's timing, and He was moving. We had to make a decision to either focus on the opposition or focus on the opportunity and move forward. If we had not been willing to rent more space and hire more people, we couldn't have kept up with the growth.

I can tell you for sure that doubt tried to stop me. I heard things like, "Joyce, you're getting in over your head"; "That's too much money to spend"; "What if the increase doesn't continue?" But rather than settle for safe, we stepped out in faith. We decided to keep pressing forward, trusting that God would provide everything we need. And you know what? That's exactly what He did!

We certainly don't want to move in the flesh or out of God's timing, but when God is moving, you can't be afraid to move with Him. In my situation, I had a choice to be led by my head or follow the leading of the Holy Spirit. Faith and adventure go hand in hand. When you stand in faith and follow God's leading, it's always an adventure. He will take you higher and farther than you could ever have gone on your own!

Your Adventure with God

Isaiah 41:10 (NKJV) says, *"Fear not, for I am with you."* Don't let the fear of something different keep you from the joy of something new. God is with you and He is going to help you. Instead of thinking about how worrisome it is to try something different, to break out of your comfort zone and shake things up, think about how wonderful it is when God does something new in your life. Adventure isn't something meant to intimidate you—it's something to invigorate you!

> *Don't let the fear of something different keep you from the joy of something new.*

Life with God is an adventure! Abraham lived with adventure,

Gideon lived with adventure, Esther lived with adventure, David lived with adventure, Paul lived with adventure…and Jesus did too. Ask God to make your story an exciting one. Whether it's in your marriage, on the job, with the kids, in your free time— look for a new adventure and get ready to see God do something incredible in your life.

Some people need more adventure than others do, and if you are a person who doesn't need much, then you don't have to have adventure just for the sake of adventure. But if you are finding that your joy has disappeared and you're interested in improving your days, having an adventure from time to time might be just what you need!

Things to remember:

- A sense of adventure is crucial to enjoying the life God has given you.
- You don't have to be a daredevil or a thrill seeker to be adventurous. You can have adventures in your career, with your family, in your downtime, and even in your relationship with God.
- It's okay if you make a mistake. The important thing is that you took a step of faith, trusting God to help you.
- Adventure and faith go hand in hand.

Suggestions for Putting "Be Adventurous" into Practice

- If the idea of being adventurous is a new concept for you, start small. Get a Post-it note and write down one thing you could do today that would be more adventurous than what you normally do or experience.
- Study men and women in the Bible who stepped out in faith, choosing the adventure God had called them to. Pray and ask God to help you learn from their example.
- If you want to, start budgeting now for a big adventure—a vacation, a mission trip, an entirely new stylish wardrobe—that you could experience a year from now.
- Identify areas of your life where you have been playing it safe. Challenge yourself to do more, aim higher, and add energy to each of those areas with God's help.

CHAPTER 10

Do Something You Enjoy

It's not how much we have, but how much we enjoy, that makes happiness.

—Charles Spurgeon

Many people have a way of making things much more complicated than they need to be. They may not do it on purpose, but they do it anyway. Have you ever done that? Have you ever complicated what should be a pretty simple situation? I know I have from time to time. As a matter of fact, I think most people have. Complication takes on many forms:

- We worry and stress-out about feeling sick when all we need is a good night's sleep.
- We panic when the car breaks down...but all it needs is gas.
- Instead of letting it go, we hold a grudge against a friend who hurt our feelings—but they don't even know what they did that offended us.
- We think of all the reasons why God could never love us instead of just believing what His Word says is true: He loves us unconditionally.
- We spend hundreds of dollars on exercise equipment we'll never use when all we need to do is go outside and take a walk.

Like I said, we have a tendency to make things complicated.

Well, this chapter is my official protest to overcomplication. And it's a chapter I've been excited to work on since I first started planning this book. I love keeping things practical, and it doesn't get more practical than this: If you want to make every day better, don't be complicated; just *do something you enjoy*! Rent a funny movie, go outside and take in the sunshine, stop by the frozen yogurt shop on the way home from work, go for a jog with a friend, have a cup of coffee and relax—have some fun and enjoy the life Jesus came to give you.

You might think, *Joyce, that doesn't sound very responsible. I have things to do. I have obligations. I can't just go through each day doing what sounds like fun.* I'm not suggesting that you stop meeting your obligations and responsibilities, but I am suggesting that you add flavor to your life by working in some things that you enjoy. Resist the temptation to go through life as a martyr. You don't have to be burdened and overwhelmed twenty-four hours a day in order to be a success or to get approval. Work is an important part of life, but life is about more than work. If the only time you feel good about yourself is when you are working, then you're making life too complicated.

> If the only time you feel good about yourself is when you are working, then you're making life too complicated.

I am a very task-oriented person, and I actually really like going to work and getting things done; however, the Lord showed me a long time ago the importance of slowing down and making time to do some of the other things I enjoy doing. I've been writing today for several hours, but about three different times I have taken short breaks. Once I got something to drink and went and sat on the deck for ten minutes in the sunshine. Little things sometimes help the most. Jesus said in John 10:10:

> The thief comes only in order to steal and kill and destroy.
> **I came that they may have and enjoy life,** and have it in abundance (to the full, till it overflows).

Isn't that amazing? Jesus came that you and I may enjoy our lives—it's really that simple! In the craziness of the world, throughout the busyness of each day, in spite of the difficulties you face, regardless of the circumstances you find yourself in, no matter how much responsibility you have...God wants you to have some fun. God's will is for you to enjoy your life.

In case that's news to you, or if you're not really sure where to start, let me give you some ways to do something you enjoy:

1. Identify what you enjoy doing.

Do you know that most people would hesitate if you asked them, "What do you do for fun?" You'd get a lot of replies that started with "Ummmm..." or "Well, let me thiiiiiink..." or even "I'm not sure. Can I get back to you?" The fact is that many people are so busy and so burdened that they stopped having fun a long time ago...and they don't know how to start again. I was that person a few years ago, and I had to actually *learn* how to enjoy life.

I now have several different things I enjoy doing when I have some downtime. I like to watch really good movies, I love spending time with my children and grandchildren, I like to go shopping, I like the smell of a great candle, and I do enjoy spending time with good friends, especially the ones who make me laugh!

Now, I'm a person with a full calendar, and I can't do these things all the time, but I've learned that if I make time for the things I enjoy, I'm actually more productive when I'm working. It's all about balance.

What are some things you enjoy? In order to *do* what you enjoy, you have to *know* what you enjoy. If you like to go to the gym, can you find time to go more often? If you enjoy playing music, when was the last time you played? If you love a good cup of coffee, why not sit down and enjoy that next cup rather than gulping it down on your way to work? Identify what you enjoy... and then let yourself enjoy it.

> In order to do what you enjoy, you have to know what you enjoy.

2. Don't wait on "when."

So many people have the mind-set that they will be really happy and enjoy life *when*. *When* they go on vacation, *when* the kids are older, *when* they get higher on the ladder of success at work, *when* they get married—the list could go on and on.

I can relate to this because there was a time when even though I really loved being in the ministry, I wasn't enjoying the daily responsibilities and activities it involved. I had to learn to live in the moment and enjoy what God was doing in me and through me *now*, not when the conference was over or when I could go on vacation. I really want you to get this: God wants you to enjoy your life *now*, not *when*.

- You may be having a tough day, but don't wait until another day to find some joy. Look for something good in each day.

- You may not have any extra money to spend right now, but that doesn't mean you can't do something you enjoy. Find an affordable (or free) option and have a blast!
- You may have a two-year-old who makes you feel like you want to run away from home right now, but try to settle down and enjoy this stage in their life, because it will only happen once.

And if you feel like you're absolutely way too busy to enjoy something right now...

3. Schedule/plan time to do what you enjoy.

Perhaps you really can't stop what you're doing right now and go have some fun, but let's be honest—for most of us, if we don't actually schedule some time to do something fun or relaxing, it will never happen. There is always a new meeting, an unexpected phone call, an errand to run, or a pressing emergency that pushes anything fun or enjoyable to the back burner. I've found that a good practice is to actually use your calendar as your ally, instead of letting it become your enemy. I've

> Use your calendar as your ally, instead of letting it become your enemy.

learned to schedule time to do the things I enjoy. Finish what you are committed to right now, but start right away planning some fun time into your future. Even knowing a break is coming soon will help you now.

I once heard a businesswoman say that someone asked her what she was doing on a certain day. She replied, "Hold on, let me check my schedule. Oh, I'm not doing anything on that day."

The other person said, "Great. I need to set up an appointment with you." She answered politely but firmly, "Oh, I don't think you understand. That day won't work for me. My calendar says I'm not doing anything." That's a perfect example of what it looks like to schedule some time to step away from the routines of your busy life, relax, and take time to do what you enjoy.

4. Enjoy the little things.

Dwight L. Moody said, "There are many of us who are willing to do great things for the Lord, but few of us are willing to do little things."[4] This is so true! And I think it's also true in the things we enjoy. Most of us have no problem enjoying the big things, like banner days and exciting announcements, but we often miss out on the little things.

Frequently, it's the little things in life that can bring us the most joy: a baby's laugh, a beautiful sunrise, a delicious dinner, a funny movie, a good conversation. I have laughed harder just being with a couple of friends than I have at a lot of movies that were advertised as comedies! Dave and I laugh a lot together, especially in the morning. It seems to be Dave's special time to tease me. Sometimes I am trying to stay focused and get something done and he delights in annoying me, and we both end up laughing! Your marriage will last if you learn to laugh together.

We don't all have big things available to us, but we do have little things we can appreciate and enjoy. If you're having a not-so-good day, take a walk through your house and then thank God that you can walk. Go turn on your hot and cold running water at the sink or bathtub and then thank God that you have plenty of clean water and that you didn't have to walk three hours to get water like many people in the world have to do.

Whatever you do, don't just sit around and be unhappy all day. Be proactive and do something that can make your day better.

5. *Take responsibility for your own happiness.*

I've learned that you cannot count on someone else to make you happy. You must take responsibility for your own happiness. There was a time when I would feel sorry for myself if Dave went to play golf the day after one of our big conferences. I wanted him to go shopping or watch a movie with me. But God showed me that we have different ways of relaxing and unwinding. By keeping our expectations of each other real, we can be free to do what we really enjoy.

Every single day is filled with all kinds of situations that could upset you—things like losing your car keys or getting caught in a traffic jam. But you can choose to be at peace and in control. You can take responsibility for your own happiness, rather than giving that responsibility to other people or outside situations.

It's Really Pretty Simple

Wow! Think about what we've accomplished in this chapter (one of my favorite chapters so far). We've cut through the clutter of complication and come to the simple but powerful realization that one of the best things we can do to enjoy every day is to take time to do what we enjoy. And on top of that, we've discovered five specific steps to help us make space for those things in our lives. I hope it's been a helpful chapter for you and one that you can come back to whenever life gets too busy and your days get too bogged down.

Remember, enjoying the life Jesus came to give you isn't that complicated. If you enjoy walking outside...go for a walk. If you enjoy knitting...relax and knit. If you enjoy baking...by all means, bake (and eat what you bake). If you enjoy reading... well, good for you, you're reading right now! Whatever it is you love to do...make some time to do it as often as you can. It's really pretty simple, isn't it?

Things to remember:

- If you want to make every day better, *do something you enjoy*! Have some fun and enjoy the life Jesus came to give you.
- You don't have to be burdened and overwhelmed twenty-four hours a day in order to be a success or to get approval. Work is an important part of life, but life is about more than work.
- Don't wait on *when* to do something you enjoy. Make the most of today.
- For most people, if they don't actually schedule some time to do something fun or relaxing, it will never happen.
- You can (and should) be the person who takes responsibility for your happiness.

Suggestions for Putting "Do Something You Enjoy" into Practice

- Don't wait. Don't put it off. Take at least thirty minutes today (and longer if desired) to do something you really, really enjoy.
- Make a list of things you enjoy—big things, and lots of little things. Start putting checkmarks behind the ones you actually take time to do.
- Ask yourself these two questions: "When was the last time I did something I really enjoy?" and "How often does that actually happen?" If you're not satisfied with the answers, be determined to do something to change it.

CHAPTER 11

Living Truly

All truths are easy to understand once they are discovered; the point is to discover them.

—Galileo Galilei

I once heard a fable or parable that went something like this:

One day, the devil was walking around with one of his cohorts. They were surveying mankind, wondering whom their next target would be, when they saw a young man stoop down and pick up a shiny but broken object.

"What did he find?" asked the devil's lackey.

"A piece of the truth," replied the devil.

"Should we be worried? Does it bother you that he has found a piece of truth?" asked the demon.

"No," Satan replied. "As long as he only has the partial truth, it will do him more harm than good."

Partial, or diluted, truth can be very dangerous. It can bind us up in condemnation, convincing us that we are inferior or unworthy. We may not realize it at the time, but partial truth clouds our judgment, deceives our heart, steals our joy, and twists our motives. For example:

- If you've heard the truth that God loves you but believe He only loves you when you *earn* His love, you've fallen victim to partial truth. You'll go through life beating yourself up, trying to earn something that has been freely given (see Romans 5:8; 1 John 4:19).

- If you've heard the truth that the devil is your enemy and you go through life afraid of him and terrified of how or when he might attack you, you're living in the oppression of partial truth. We do have an enemy, but he is nothing you have to fear. God is greater! (See 1 John 4:4.) We can resist the devil and he has to flee! (See James 4:7.)

- If you understand the importance of relationships but go through life trying to please everyone around you in order to get them to like you, you're suffering from a partial truth. Friendships and strong relationships are important and can be very beneficial, but you don't have to change who you are to please someone else. Be yourself—the unique, valuable person God created you to be. A true friend will love you for you (see Psalm 139:14).

These examples, and many others like them, demonstrate why the devil wants you to live a life that is only partially based on truth. If you settle for less than the full truth, you'll always be frustrated, discouraged, and miserable.

But a life based on full truth is a life that you can truly enjoy!

There is nothing more powerful than complete truth, or "living truly." The truth of God's Word, the truth of who God says you are, the truth of healing and freedom, the truth of forgiveness and redemption— these are life-changing, revolutionary truths! When you know the truth (the full truth) and determine to live your life in the power of that truth, you no longer

> *Rather than being a confused victim, living truly makes you a confident victor in Christ.*

fall for the enemy's schemes. Rather than being a confused victim, living truly makes you a confident victor in Christ.

Just look at what the Bible says about truth and how that truth can affect your life:

> And you will know the Truth, and the Truth will set you free.
>
> John 8:32

> Jesus said to him, I am the Way and the Truth and the Life; no one comes to the Father except by (through) Me.
>
> John 14:6

> The Lord is near to all who call upon Him, to all who call upon Him sincerely and in truth.
>
> Psalm 145:18

And one of my personal favorites:

> Rather, let our lives lovingly express truth [in all things, speaking truly, dealing truly, **living truly**].
>
> Ephesians 4:15

Notice it doesn't say "living doubtfully," "living questionably," or "living in partial truth." Paul says that we can live in the power of God's truth—we can be "living truly."

I believe that living truly is an essential key to enjoying your life in Christ. When you learn to find truth in your identity, your relationships, and your walk with God, everything changes for the better! The condemnation of half-truths is gone. The fear that comes with deception disappears. The discouragement of partial truth is wiped away. *Living truly* is a life that brings peace, hope, and joy for all who choose it!

No More Excuses

Luke 19:1–10 tells the story of Zacchaeus the tax collector. It's a fascinating story of forgiveness and redemption, but there is another element of this story that I want to show you—something I've never heard anyone else talk about.

If you've spent much time in church, you're probably well acquainted with the brief story. Zacchaeus was an incredibly unpopular tax collector of the Jewish people. Though he himself was Jewish, he worked for the oppressive Roman Empire, funding the cruel empire by taxing his fellow countrymen, and getting rich by lining his own pockets in the process.

In Luke 19, when Jesus travels through Jericho, Zacchaeus hears about the trip and joins the crowds lining the street, hoping to get a glimpse of the much-talked-about rabbi and miracle worker. Because Zacchaeus is a short man, he can't see over the mob of people, so he climbs a tree. What a picture! A cheat, a traitor, an enemy of the state…hanging from a tree limb, hoping to meet a Savior.

This is where we pick up the story in Luke 19:5. Jesus sees Zacchaeus and tells him to climb down from the tree because He wants to go to his house for dinner. The crowd murmurs, but in that moment the crooked tax collector is changed. Without hesitation, he "stood up and solemnly declared":

> See, Lord, the half of my goods I [now] give [by way of restoration] to the poor, and if I have cheated anyone out of anything, I [now] restore four times as much.
>
> Luke 19:8

Many lessons have been taught and many sermons have been preached about Zacchaeus' turnaround. His heart change is sincere, and in the next verse, Jesus recognizes that and says that "salvation" has come to his household. But there is something else I want you to see: Zacchaeus makes no excuses.

He doesn't say, "Well, I didn't have a choice because..." or "If you only knew how much pressure I'm under..." or "I didn't have a very good home life growing up..." The cheating tax collector doesn't say any of those things. When confronted by Jesus, Zacchaeus faces his problem, owns up to his mistakes, makes restitution where possible, and vows to change.

I share that account with you from the Word of God because I believe that in order to experience a *living truly* life, we have to stop making excuses. Excuses for a poor attitude, excuses for a quick temper, excuses for a lack of initiative, excuses for that decision to quit—all of these (and more) will keep you from experiencing a joy-filled, *living truly* life. If you'll face your problems, own up to your mistakes, make restitution where possible, and decide to change, you'll be amazed at how much more you'll enjoy every single day.

I realize there are *reasons* why we mess up and fall short. I understand there are contributing factors that shape our emotions and personalities. I grew up in an abusive home and suffered from a lot of pain in life because of it, so I understand what it's like to have to overcome fears, doubts, and dysfunction in order to move forward. But you don't have to let *reasons* for your behavior become *excuses* for your behavior. You can choose to face your issues head-on and overcome your past rather than live as a prisoner of it.

> *You don't have to let* reasons *for your behavior become* excuses *for your behavior.*

You can either live an excuse-filled life or a joy-filled life—but you can't live both. I suggest you choose a joy-filled life . . . a *living truly* life, free of excuses.

- If there are issues from your past that are causing you pain, take them to God, get the help you need, and choose to face those issues head-on. *No excuses!*
- If you made a mistake, evaluate what you did wrong, learn from your mistake, and try again. *No excuses!*
- If you've been afraid to step out and try, admit you've let fear hold you back, ask for God's strength, and move forward . . . even if you feel afraid. *No excuses!*
- If you are unhappy, ask God to show you the true reason for it. You might be surprised to find it is something in your attitude that you can adjust, and then get on with the business of enjoying your day. *No excuses!*

It's only when we stop making excuses that we are going to find freedom. Zacchaeus decided to live excuse-free, and his life changed. If you make the same decision, I'm convinced you'll get the same result!

The Truth Is Greater Than Your Feelings

Henry Augustus Rowland, professor of physics at Johns Hopkins University, was once called as an expert witness at a trial. During cross-examination a lawyer demanded, "What are your qualifications as an expert witness in this case?"

The normally modest and retiring professor replied quietly, "I am the greatest living expert on the subject under discussion."

Later a friend well acquainted with Rowland's disposition

expressed surprise at the professor's uncharacteristic answer. Rowland answered, "Well, what did you expect me to do? I was under oath."[5]

Henry Augustus Rowland knew this: *He* was the expert. Anybody else testifying might be persuasive, but they wouldn't know the full truth that he knew. I share that story with you because there is only one "expert" when it comes to the case of your life—your Heavenly Father.

God created you, He knows you, and He knows the plans He has for you. It is God's Word that provides the only real truth for our lives. Living truly means seeing yourself and your situation through the prism of the Word of God. It doesn't matter what the circumstances look like, what other people say, or even how you *feel* in the moment. God is the expert, and His Word is the only truth that matters.

> Living truly means seeing yourself and your situation through the prism of the Word of God.

Much of the time, people live by their feelings. If you listen, you'll hear people talk about how they *feel* more than just about anything else. I wonder sometimes if we're serving the god of our feelings more than the God of the Bible. For example, someone says, "I don't *feel* God loves me." Well, He does. Or, "I don't *feel* I have much of a future." Well, you do. The Bible clearly says God loves us (see John 3:16) and that He has good plans for us (see Jeremiah 29:11). But when we believe the lies the enemy puts in our mind rather than the Word of God, we will *feel* like the lies are true and then live like it.

People who rely on their emotions make big mistakes when they base decisions on how they feel, rather than obeying God and what they know is the right thing to do. We have to learn how to live beyond our feelings and do what's right even when we *feel* wrong.

I will admit that I struggled in life with emotional ups and downs until I finally accepted that no matter what I think, or how I feel, or what I want or do not want, God's Word is the truth, and I have to believe it more than anything or anyone else. If you are willing to take that step of faith right now, you can say goodbye to most of your bad days! Why do I say that? Because most of the time, when we are having bad days it is because we are thinking something that doesn't agree with God's Word, feeling something that doesn't agree with God's Word, or wanting something that doesn't agree with God's Word. I had countless bad days because the devil made me think and feel guilty about something that I had repented of and God had forgiven me for and forgotten.

> For I will be merciful and gracious toward their sins and
> I will remember their deeds of unrighteousness no more.
> Hebrews 8:12

Someone recently asked me to talk to them about discipline. They wanted to exercise and make better food choices, but said they had difficulty with the discipline. This is something most of us have dealt with at times, but I have never seen Dave struggle much with discipline. If you ask him why it is not difficult for him to discipline himself, he will tell you that he sets his mind to do what he wants to do and never changes it. Dave is not an emotionally driven man and he doesn't live by how he feels. (Except when he is playing bad golf, or driving behind someone who is driving really badly. I guess we all have our limits!)

For a long time, when he told me that he just made his mind up and didn't change it, it irritated me and made me a bit angry. I recall telling him that he might not be human! I did struggle in some areas, and I continued to struggle until I learned what Dave already knew: If we want to do anything that is likely to require any type of sacrifice, we cannot ask ourselves how we *feel* about it, or what we think.

I am going to India soon for a ministry trip and I will be on a plane for a forty-two-hour round trip flight. How do I feel about that? I dare not ask myself! I have committed to go, I believe I should go, and I am going to be able to bring the Gospel to some very needy people; therefore, I am going and my feelings will just have to go along with me, whether they want to or not. To me, that is discipline.

What about you? How often do you say, "I *feel* like…" or "I don't *feel* like…" and then how many times do those feelings win out? Do your feelings dictate how you treat people? Or what you say about your situation? Do feelings run your life? Do they keep you from exercising regularly, or eating a healthy and well-balanced diet? Do they urge you to spend money that you cannot afford to spend?

If they do and you follow them, you will definitely have lots of bad days! But it doesn't have to be that way. You have choices, and you can begin exercising them today. What can you do today to help yourself? Do you have to be trapped in a bad day, or could you change it right now by doing what you *know* is the right thing to do instead of what you *feel* like doing?

You may be thinking, *Well, I can't help how I feel!* That's true; I totally agree—but don't use how you feel as an excuse not to do the right thing. You will enjoy a new level of confidence as you begin to live truly instead of emotionally!

There have been times when I have felt insecure about speaking at a conference. But I decided to trust God and have confidence that He would help me. When I stepped out to teach, the feelings of insecurity went away. There have been times when I've been angry with Dave and felt like giving him the cold shoulder, but when I decided to pray and ask God for the grace to forgive him or ask for his forgiveness, I've had the ability to treat him the way God wants me to.

I'm sure the same could be said for you. There are always going to be times when you do or don't feel a certain way, but the key here is refusing to be passive and making a conscious decision to do what's right. Set your mind to agree with God and live based on the truth of His Word. Like we all do, you will fail at times, but you can keep making more and more progress and have fewer and fewer *bad days*.

The Very Best Life

The very best life is a *living truly* life—a life that has moved out of the confusing shadows of partial truth and dwells in the light of full truth. This isn't just some life we wish for, wondering if it could possibly come true. This is the life Jesus promised! He said in John 16:13:

> But when He, the Spirit of Truth (the Truth-giving Spirit) comes, He will guide you into all the Truth (the whole, full Truth).

As you go through today...and tomorrow...and the next day, ask God to help you live a *living truly* life. Refuse to settle for partial truth, reject excuses for yourself or from others, and choose to stand on the truth of God's Word whether you feel like it or not. When you make these decisions, no enemy and no obstacle can keep you from enjoying your life more than you ever have before!

Things to remember:

- Partial or diluted truth can be very dangerous. It can trap us in condemnation, convincing us that we are inferior or unworthy of God's love and His help.
- When you learn to walk in full truth concerning your identity as God's child, everything changes for the better!
- Excuses will keep you from experiencing a joy-filled, *living truly* life.
- Are you serving the god of your feelings more than the God of the Bible?
- God created you, He knows you, and He knows the plans He has for you. It is God's Word that provides the only real truth for our lives.

Suggestions for Putting "Living Truly" into Practice

- List a few of the things you've built your life on. Are these partial truths based on your opinions or experiences, or full truths from the Word of God?
- Confront your excuses. Write down or print out an "excuse-free declaration" like the one Zacchaeus made about the kind of life he was going to live from that point on.
- Identify some feelings—such as fear, worry, or insecurity—that are currently determining your actions in life. Face those feelings and choose the truth of God's Word from this point forward.

SECTION III

Patterns to Break

...Let us strip off and throw aside every encumbrance (unnecessary weight) and that sin which so readily (deftly and cleverly) clings to and entangles us, and let us run with patient endurance and steady and active persistence the appointed course of the race that is set before us.

Hebrews 12:1

CHAPTER 12

Say No to Worry

Sorrow looks back, worry looks around, faith looks up.
—Ralph Waldo Emerson

If you came home today to find that your house had been infested with insects—I'm talking about large, disgusting, germ-carrying bugs—what would you do? Would you coexist with the gross insects? Would you let them scurry around the living room, hoping that they would eventually go away? Or would you take immediate steps to eradicate them?

If this happened to me, I can tell you right now I would not be happy. I would take immediate and aggressive action. After screaming and running out of the house, I'd probably call every exterminator within fifty miles. And then I'd definitely make Dave take me to the nearest hotel until the problem was solved. There is no way I would stay in a house overrun by bugs!

You know, it's interesting: We will go to great lengths to rid our homes of harmful, disgusting pests, but yet we will allow our lives to be full of harmful, disgusting patterns. Why is that?

I want you to get this picture in your mind: dread, fear, anxiety, stress, and worry—these are the emotional insects that are scurrying around the corners of our souls. Like bugs, these feelings of worry are unhealthy, unsightly, and prefer the darkness. Rather than coexisting with worry and anxiety, or just hoping they will

> *Rather than coexisting with worry and anxiety, or just hoping they will go away, we should take immediate and aggressive action.*

go away, we should take immediate and aggressive action. We should say emphatically, "There is no way I'm going to allow my life to be overrun by worry!"

The Problem of Worry

If you are worried about anything today, it will drain the energizing life and joy out of the day that God wants you to have. Feeling uneasy, troubled, or worried seems to plague so many. It's human nature to be concerned about the difficulties in our world and in our personal lives, but if we're not careful, those concerns will become fears and unreasonable worries.

I've often said that worry is like a rocking chair—it's always in motion but it never gets you anywhere. Worry is in direct contradiction to faith, and it steals our peace, physically wears us out, and can even make us sick. Worry is totally useless because it never makes anything better. When we worry, we torment ourselves—we're doing the devil's job for him!

If worry is so harmful, why do we keep doing it? And what causes it to be so prevalent? Well, the biggest cause of worry is not trusting God to take care of the various situations in our lives. Too often we put our trust in our own abilities, believing that we can figure out how to take care of our own problems better than God can. Yet after all our worry and effort to go it alone, we come up short, unable to bring about suitable solutions.

At a young age, I discovered firsthand that people hurt people, so I didn't trust others. I tried to take care of myself, deciding not to depend on anyone who would hurt or disappoint me. But my life was filled with anxiety and worry. Too often our experiences in the world teach us to go it alone, and even after we become Christians, it takes a long time to overcome it. Anytime we're depending on ourselves

> *We'll never be worry-free until we become God-dependent!*

rather than trusting God, worry is the natural result. It's challenging to learn how to trust God, but we eventually must learn that trying to take care of everything ourselves is too big a task. We'll never be worry-free until we become God-dependent!

Let Go of That Care... Give It to God

One of my favorite Scriptures is 1 Peter 5:6–7. It says:

> Therefore humble yourselves [demote, lower yourselves in your own estimation] under the mighty hand of God, that in due time He may exalt you, casting the whole of your care [all your anxieties, all your worries, all your concerns, once and for all] on Him, for He cares for you affectionately and cares about you watchfully.

What a wonderful Scripture! God doesn't just invite us to give our cares to Him—He *instructs* us to! With that in mind, why would we hold on to our worries, our problems, and our cares? The surest way to find joy in our lives is to follow God's guidelines, and they require that we quit worrying. And according to 1 Peter 5:6–7, there are two ways to do it: (1) Humble ourselves, and (2) Cast our care on Him.

Many of our struggles are perpetuated because we're too proud to ask for help, or we do ask for help, but we refuse to let go. But here are five words I want you to remember: The humble get the help. So if your way isn't working, why not try God's way? We'll

The humble get the help.

always be better off when we lean on God and ask for His help. But as long as we try to do everything ourselves, God will let us—God won't force us to do things His way. And He will only take care of our problems and worries when we let them go and give them to Him. Either we're going to do it or God's going to do it, but both of us aren't going to do it.

So the cure for worry is humbling ourselves before God in the realization that we are simply not capable of solving all of our own problems, casting our cares on Him, and trusting Him. Instead of making ourselves miserable trying to figure everything out on our own, God wants us to place our trust in Him and enter into His rest, totally abandoning ourselves to His care. When we simply trust God and let go of our worries, He'll bring a harvest of blessings into our lives. I admit that it is often scary to let go of things because sometimes it takes awhile before God acts, but He is never too late! We obtain the promises of God by faith and patience!

A Worry-Free Attitude for a Worry-Free Life

I've learned that my attitude has a lot to do with living a worry-free life. There will always be situations that cause us concern, but with God's help, we can live above all of it and enjoy life. Our worries are caused by the way we approach our circumstances and the attitude we have toward them. It was a turning point for me when I realized that the world will probably never change, but I can learn how to change the way I go about handling tough situations.

Too many times we meditate on the problem—rolling it over and over in our mind, trying to figure out how things should work out. It's almost like we're telling God, "I kind of think You need my help, and I'm not sure You can take care of this situation, Lord." We need to realize

> We need to realize that God doesn't need our help!

that God doesn't need our help! Trusting Him means we give up worry and anxiety, choosing instead to enter into His rest with simple childlike faith.

I want to be honest and say that I fully realize that learning how to totally trust God is a process in our lives. We usually begin with baby steps. We trust God *"for"* something we want, and if we see Him provide, we are encouraged to trust Him for more. But the time comes when He wants us to transition from simply trusting Him "for" things to trusting Him *"in"* things.

When we give a care to God and refuse to worry, He may show us something He wants us to do, and it might be something we would have never even thought of. When we follow His lead, the problem gets solved without all the misery we would have had doing it our own way.

God doesn't always move in the amount of time we would like Him to move in, so waiting stretches and tests our faith! It is all in the plan of God. He wants to help us with our situation, but even more than that, He wants to help us learn how to have peace at all times—in little problems and big ones, when God moves quickly and when we have to wait a long time. Nothing is more wonderful than peace, and it comes by refusing to worry and learning to trust God.

Goodbye, Worry—Hello, Peace

I've seen so many lives consumed and ruined by worry. For many years, I was the ultimate example of how destructive worry can be. But over time, through study of the Word and by the grace of God, I've learned the uselessness of worry and the joy of trusting God. I'm not perfect—there are still days when worry creeps in—but I've come a long way. *And I'm determined to keep going!*

I want you to get to the point in your life where you can say the same thing—"Worry no longer has a hold on me!" Like everything else we've talked about so far in this book, you might not be able to master this by the end of the day...but you can *start* it by the end of the day. You can make today the day you started saying no to worry!

And in those times when you are tempted to settle back into that old habit of anxiety and worry, just remember the picture I gave you at the beginning of the chapter. Worry, fear, and anxiety are the insects that try to scurry around the corners of your soul. Turn the lights on, call the exterminator, and take aggressive action against those pests today!

Things to remember:

- We will go to great lengths to rid our homes of harmful, disgusting pests, but we'll allow our lives to be full of harmful, disgusting patterns. It's time to make a change!
- Worry is in direct contradiction to faith, and it steals our peace, physically wears us out, and can even make us sick.
- God doesn't just invite us to give our cares to Him—He instructs us to!
- Learn to trust God "in" things, rather than just "for" things.
- There will always be situations that cause us concern, but with God's help, we can live above all of it and enjoy life.

Suggestions for Putting "Say No to Worry" into Practice

- Give yourself a new title: "The Worry Exterminator." Every time you feel yourself getting worried, roll up your sleeves and get to work destroying that worry.
- Write down the things you are worried about, and then ball up the paper. Physically "cast" those worries into the wastebasket as a symbol of your casting those cares upon the Lord.
- Ask God if there are areas in your life where you have been too proud to lean on Him for help. Humble yourself and depend on Him to give you the help and the strength you need to move forward.

CHAPTER 13

Slow Down

For fast-acting relief, try slowing down.

—Lily Tomlin

The busy, hectic pace of life is one of the major culprits that lessens our joy and decreases our peace. For many people, their lifestyles just aren't manageable. We're like a hamster on a wheel, running faster and faster but not accomplishing anything except exhausting ourselves. It seems like we're doing more and more but enjoying life less and less.

It would probably be easier to solve this problem if we had someone else to blame—you know, an outside force, an external villain. But the truth is that many times the blame lies with us. *We're* the ones tied to our phones. *We're* the ones pressing for more. *We're* the ones texting, calling, and emailing all at the same time. *We're* the ones speeding from one appointment to another. You and I—we're the ones to blame.

You might not want to believe that, but it's true. Let me give you a little quiz to see if you're living a "sped up, plugged in" kind of life.

- Do you check your phone *first thing* in the morning for texts, emails, news updates, or social media notifications?
- Do you get frustrated when the person in front of you is driving so slowly . . . but they are actually driving the speed limit?

- Do you find yourself lying in bed, thinking of all the things you want to get done the next day and feeling pressured?
- Do you choose your restaurants or coffee shops depending on which ones have Wi-Fi?
- Are you a constant multitasker?
- Do you put your phone on the table in front of you when you're having a conversation with someone?
- Do you have more "apps" than friends?

If you answered yes to a majority of these questions, you probably need to rethink some things and consider slowing down. We don't enjoy any day we have if we are in such a rush that we barely even know what is going on around us.

I know from personal experience exactly what it's like to live a fast-paced life. I am on the go a lot, and I am usually thinking three steps ahead. Rushing, and not keeping my mind on what I am doing, actually causes me to lose time. I make mistakes and do really silly things that require time and effort to correct. The other day I poured the water for my coffee pot into the area where the coffee beans go for grinding! It was a huge mess and took

> When we take the time to slow down, live in the moment, and occasionally unplug, we enjoy life so much more.

time to clean up. When we take the time to slow down, live in the moment, and occasionally unplug, we enjoy life so much more.

There is nothing wrong with being on the go. And there is certainly nothing bad about having and enjoying modern technology that keeps you connected to your friends and to the world. But as I've said before in this book, balance is key. Excess—too much of anything—can be destructive. That's why it's important to make the choice to regularly slow down and unplug. If you are having a bad day and you picked this book up today to see if anything in it would help you, and if you happened to turn to this chapter... maybe, just maybe, God is telling you to slow down. You may not be enjoying your life because you miss most of it by rushing!

Let me give you five important ways to slow down and unplug:

1. Resist the temptation to overcommit or overextend.

When you think about your life, do you find that you have too much to do? Without a doubt, this has to be the number one complaint I hear today. When I ask people how they are, the most common response is, "Joyce, I'm busy!" Common sense tells us that God isn't going to stress us out and lead us to do more than we can do with peace and joy. Therefore, unless we are the ones overcommitting and trying to do too many things, we should be able to do all that we truly need to do, and do so with enjoyment.

So the question becomes: Do you need to say no more often?

> Sometimes trying to keep other people happy can make us very unhappy.

We should be sure when our heart says *no* that our mouth isn't saying *yes*. Sometimes trying to keep other people happy can make us very unhappy. This is an area where we really need to be careful, especially if we don't like to "let people down." Being a people-pleaser is a sure way to live an overcommitted life.

We also need to be sure that we're not overextending ourselves by trying to do too many things we *want* to do, whether it's part of God's plan for us or not. If we're doing something God hasn't approved, He's under no obligation to give us energy to do it. I believe one of the major reasons why many people are living overly busy lives is because they're going their own way instead of following God's plan. We need to ask for God's guidance as to what we're to be involved in and where we're to expend our energy. We must learn to say yes when God says yes and no when He says no. God will never lead you to do so much that it frustrates you and causes you not to enjoy the day.

2. Check your pace of life.

If you like to go to the gym and run on a treadmill, you know that treadmills are equipped to help you check the pace you're running and the rate at which your heart is beating. It's important to keep an eye on this to optimize your workout and do so in a healthy way.

Well, in the same way, it's important that you check the pace of your life. If you keep an eye on how quickly you're moving through life and how that movement is affecting your physical, mental, and emotional health, you will optimize your life!

Whose pace are you moving at? Is it the pace God has set for you, or someone else's pace? Are you burning out from trying to keep up with everyone else? Are you living under the stress of competition and comparison? Are you a perfectionist with unrealistic goals? If you have difficulty slowing down, I know exactly how you feel. This is

> Whose pace are you moving at? Is it the pace God has set for you, or someone else's pace?

something I have been dealing with for a long time, and although I have improved, I am certainly not where I need to be. I have to remind myself, "Joyce, slow down!" The other day I was eating— I tend to do that too fast, too—and I didn't chew a piece of food properly before swallowing it. It got lodged in my esophagus and I thought for a brief minute that I might have to go to the

emergency room! I did some intense praying along with promis-
ing God that I would seriously make an effort to slow down when
I am eating. It actually frightened me and I thought, *Well, this is
the height of ridiculous.* It is simply a bad habit, but I can make a
new healthy habit with God's help, and so can you.

I urge you to check your pace of life and be honest in your
evaluation. I have a friend who is with me a lot who walks and
moves very slowly, and I tend to get annoyed and think, *Do you
really have to move that slowly?* But maybe God has put her in my
life to be a constant reminder to me that I need to change my
pace. And maybe she isn't really even that slow—maybe I am just
way too fast.

I believe you can be successful, content, and happy, but it will
require some decisions—possibly some radical decisions. Allow
God's Spirit to lead you away from a way too fast-paced lifestyle
and into one with a healthier pace.

3. Follow the guidance of the Holy Spirit.

Some of the decisions that we make are proof that we need help
in guiding our lives properly, and that is exactly why God sent
His Holy Spirit to live in us.

Romans 7:6 says we are to be led by the "prompting" of the
Spirit. There have been several times when I was tired and the
Holy Spirit prompted me to slow down and rest. But rather than
obey, I continued to push myself to go out or to have company.
Then I ended up *exhausted*, instead of just being tired.

I remember one specific time when I'd been shopping for several hours and was getting very tired. I had only purchased about
half of the items I intended to buy, so I kept pressing on. The
prompting of the Spirit within me was telling me to stop and

go home, but because I hadn't accomplished my goal, I didn't. Although the other things I intended to get weren't immediate needs, I didn't want to leave until I accomplished the goal I had set for myself. As I pushed myself to the point of exhaustion, it became difficult for me to think clearly. I then began to become impatient with other people. Even after I finally went home, I was out of sorts, and it affected my time with my family.

If I had obeyed the prompting of the Spirit and gone home to slow down and rest, I would have enjoyed a good day instead of ending up with bad one! We can avoid many difficult situations simply by obeying the Holy Spirit's prompting. Obedience is exalting God above our own natural, selfish desires. So I ask you: *Are you exhausted . . . or is Jesus exalted?*

4. Turn off your electronic devices for a few minutes every day.

It's a very interesting and exciting time we live in. The wonders of technology have made us more connected to friends, family, and the rest of the world than ever before. We can send pictures, tweet thoughts, and have a video chat without ever leaving the house. But some of the very things that make our mobile devices helpful can also make them harmful. The fact that we can be reached at any time means we are always "on the clock." And it seems like we're constantly distracted and consumed by our phone, tablet, or laptop.

Even Jesus got away from the busy demands of life—He "withdrew" to lonely places and prayed (see Luke 5:16). That means He avoided the crowds and stepped away from the disciples. It was important for Him

> *If Jesus were walking the earth today, I have a feeling He would turn off His phone from time to time.*

to slow down, even if it was just for a few minutes. If Jesus were walking the earth today, I have a feeling He would turn off His phone from time to time. I can't really imagine Jesus pausing His prayer so He could post a picture of the sky to His Instagram page.

I'm sure you have a lot going on, and I have no doubt that your electronic devices are helpful and valuable in your life. I'm not suggesting that they are bad or that you shouldn't have them. But I am saying that if you're not careful, your electronics can begin to own you, rather than you owning them. So why don't you consider dedicating a little time each day to turn off the electronics, or leave them someplace where you cannot see or hear them—totally unplug. Use that time to relax, to reflect, to breathe, or to give thanks. Not one of us is so important that we must be available every moment of every day.

5. Enjoy the moment—live in the now.

One final way to slow down and develop peace is to learn to live "in the now." We can spend a lot of time trying to make up for the past or working for the future, but we can't accomplish anything unless our mind is focused on today. There is no way you can enjoy today while you are thinking about tomorrow. Today matters!

I believe there is something special in each day that we should not miss, and the only way to ensure that we won't miss it is if we learn to fully enter into what we are doing each moment of the day.

Enjoying the moment and living in the now are priceless decisions. It's an attitude that says, "I'm thankful for this moment God has given me," and this attitude brings peace and contentment.

But it takes effort, because focusing is something it seems we have forgotten how to do. I read that the average attention span of an adult has plummeted from twelve minutes a decade ago to five minutes today. I also read that Microsoft did a study and found that our attention span is less than that of a goldfish! A goldfish can focus for nine seconds, while most adults can only make it eight seconds. I don't know for sure how accurate these statistics are, but one thing is for sure: We are going to miss most of what is going on around us if we don't slow down and learn once more how to focus on the moment we are in.

Put It to the Test

If you're like me—busy and always on the go—you may have even read this chapter too fast to realize that God is trying to speak to you through it. Or you might be thinking, *Joyce, these five ways to slow down sound good, but I just don't think I can slow down; I just have too much to do.* Or perhaps you, like me, have tried to slow down before and it didn't last very long.

Let's take it one day at a time and ask the Holy Spirit to show us anytime we are moving too fast. As soon as we become aware that we are rushing or hurrying, we can slow down right then, and even if we have to do it a hundred times every day, each time we do, we are making progress toward forming a new and healthy habit.

Why not take a break right now from reading and take a walk through your home (if you are at home), doing it slowly enough to actually look at all the lovely things you have in your home. Some of them are gifts you have been given, some are things you have spent a lot of money on, and perhaps you haven't even noticed them for a long, long time. Go take some time to enjoy them!

Things to remember:

- The busy, hectic pace of life is one of the major culprits that lessens our joy and decreases our peace.
- There is nothing wrong with being on the go. And there is certainly nothing bad about having and enjoying modern technology that keeps you connected to your friends and to the world. But balance is key. Excess—too much of anything—can be destructive.
- Ask for God's guidance as to what you're to be involved in and where you're to expend your energy.
- We can avoid many difficult situations simply by obeying the Holy Spirit's prompting.
- Why not dedicate a few minutes each day to turn off the electronics—totally unplug? Use that time to relax, to reflect, or to pray.

Suggestions for Putting "Slow Down" into Practice

- Make a "Top 10" list. What are the top 10 things in your week that cause you to rush and hurry the most? What can you do about some of these things? Are there creative ways to slow down and be at peace?
- Take twenty minutes today to unplug—no television, no phone, no tablet or computer. Use those minutes to rest, pray, relax, and reflect.
- Take it one day at a time and learn how to enjoy each thing you do.

CHAPTER 14

Reject Negativity

My dear friend, clear your mind of "can't."

—Samuel Johnson

You and I have more choices in life than we realize. We might not be able to choose everything we experience on a given day—the weather, our job assignments, the disposition of others around us, what takes place in the news—but we *do* get to choose how we *respond* to those experiences. I recently came across a great reminder about the power of our choices:

> I woke up early today, excited over all I get to do. I have responsibilities to fulfill—my job is to choose what kind of day I am going to have.
>
> Today I can complain because the weather is rainy or I can be thankful that the grass is getting watered for free.
>
> Today I can feel sad that I don't have more money or I can be glad that my finances encourage me to plan my purchases wisely and guide me away from waste.
>
> Today I can cry because roses have thorns or I can celebrate that thorns have roses.
>
> Today I can mourn my lack of friends or I can excitedly embark upon a quest to discover new relationships.

Today I can whine because I have to go to work or I can shout for joy because I have a job to do.

Today I can murmur dejectedly because I have to do housework or I can appreciate that I have a place to call home.

Today stretches ahead of me, waiting to be shaped. And here I am, the sculptor who gets to do the shaping. What today will be like is up to me. I get to choose what kind of day I will have![6]

I love this outlook on life! Sure, there are lots of negative things that happen around us, but we don't have to focus on the nega-tive…we can choose to see the positive! This is not just a "good idea"—this is God's will for our lives. Philippians 4:8 says:

Whatever is true, whatever is worthy of reverence and is honorable and seemly, whatever is just, whatever is pure, whatever is lovely and lovable, whatever is kind and winsome and gracious, if there is any virtue and excellence, if there is anything worthy of praise, think on and weigh and take account of these things [fix your minds on them].

Those adjectives—"true," "honorable," "pure," "lovely," "kind," and so on—are all positive things. God instructs us to fix our minds on the good things in our lives—not the bad. There is no getting around this truth: Your outlook on life determines what kind of life you will have!

I was taught to be negative when I was growing up. I lived in an abusive atmosphere with negative people, alcoholism, fear, and lots of arguing. As a result, I developed an attitude that went something like this: *It's better to expect nothing good than to expect something good and be disappointed when it doesn't happen.* It wasn't until I was an adult that I realized negativity was a destructive force in my life. I wanted my circumstances to be different, but eventually I learned that God wanted *me* to be different because even when something good did happen, I ruined it, wondering how long it would take for something to go wrong.

> I wanted my circumstances to be different, but eventually I learned that God wanted me to be different.

I am so grateful I don't constantly live with negative thinking any longer, and I feel certain that if I can change, anybody can change!

Negativity sucks the energy out of life. It actually drains our physical energy and steals our joy. There are no negative people who are going to have a good day today! It is simply not possible.

Choose Hope

Each of us is faced daily with negative things and people, but we can choose to reject a negative outlook, and with God's help, we can believe that good things are happening all around us if we will only take the time to see them. We can live lives filled with hope.

Hope is more than wishful thinking. Hope is a favorable and confident expectation; it's an expectant attitude that something good is going to happen and things will work out, no matter what situation we're facing. The more we choose hope, the better our lives will be. Samuel Smiles, a renowned nineteenth-century Scottish author, once said, "Hope is like the sun, which, as we journey toward it, casts the shadow of our burden behind us."[7] And he was 100 percent right. Hope dispels the darkness and gives us the strength to believe for something better. You don't have to wait for someone to come and give you hope, you can decide to have all of the hope you want right now. All you need to do is change your thinking!

One of my favorite ways to think of hope comes from Zechariah 9:12. This Scripture says, *"Return to the stronghold [of security and prosperity], you **prisoners of hope**; even today do I declare that I will restore double your former prosperity to you."*

I really like that phrase *prisoners of hope*. Think about it: A prisoner of hope is surrounded by hope. He has no other option—hope is his entire environment. And when times are tough or you're dealing with disappointment, a prisoner of hope will rise up in faith and say, "God, I praise You, and I believe You're working on this situation and working in me. I'm a prisoner of hope! My faith, trust, and hope are all in You!"

I am convinced that God can and will help each of us become as positive as He is! Just imagine how wonderful that will be. Do you know that God has never had even one negative thought about you? What if we could say that about our thoughts for ourselves, or others? Being around negativity is actually annoying to me now, but I once was so negative that if I accidentally thought even two positive thoughts in succession, my mind rebelled. It never ceases to amaze me how much God can change us. It is one of the greatest miracles we can ever witness! His Word says that He gives us a new nature, and puts His Spirit within us (see 2 Corinthians 5:17; 1 Corinthians 2:12). So why is it so hard to actually believe that we can learn to behave in an entirely new way?

Choose the Positive over the Negative Every Time

Just because a negative thought pops into your head, you don't have to dwell on it. You have a choice to make: *Am I going to sit here and focus on this negative idea...or am I going to choose something positive instead?* This is true in every area of your life. In your thoughts, your words, your actions, your attitude, your relationships—you can *choose* to be a positive person. Here are three steps to take when choosing the positive over the negative:

1. Identify your obstacles of negativity.

Have you ever doubted that anything good was going to happen to you? Maybe you've even said things like, "I never get any good breaks," or "Always the bridesmaid, never the bride." These thoughts are obstacles in your mind, and simply recognizing them will pave the way to your freedom. As Christians, we can learn to fight for our thoughts. 2 Corinthians 10:5 says:

> [We] refute arguments and theories and reasonings and every proud and lofty thing that sets itself up against the [true] knowledge of God; and we lead every thought and purpose away captive into the obedience of Christ (the Messiah, the Anointed One).

Our minds don't automatically come into agreement with God's plans; we will deal with negative thoughts at times. But we can choose to bring any negative thoughts "captive into the obedience of Christ."

> *We can choose to bring any negative thoughts "captive into the obedience of Christ."*

We need God's help in recognizing any negativity in our lives. Sometimes we have been that way for so long that we don't even realize it is not the right way to be. We may think, *Well, of course I am negative. Everything in the world is negative!*

How can I be positive with so much violence, war, crime, and dishonesty all around me? That is exactly the point! It is all around us, but it doesn't have to get "in" us unless we allow it to.

2. Regularly practice positivity.

Once you've identified obstacles of negative thinking and negative expectations, the next step is to start practicing being positive in all kinds of situations. Cheer up, have a good attitude, laugh, encourage others, get your hopes up—these are all ways to practice positivity. I saw a sign one time that said, "There are 86,400 seconds in a day—have you used one of them to smile?"

Even when you're going through a difficult time in life, you can have a positive outlook. The most positive people still deal with disappointing situations. The difference is that they have learned to trust God and enjoy life no matter what happens. We can choose to worry or to trust God, and my experience has taught me that worry changes nothing; therefore, trusting God must be better! If you want to have a joyful attitude, it all begins with trusting God. God is working on your problems, so why not go ahead and enjoy your day!

3. Declare God's promises.

A positive life is not only thinking positive, God-honoring thoughts. It's just as important to speak positive, faith-filled words. Nearly everything God has brought me through has happened by believing and confessing His Word. That's why I encourage you to not only purposely think right thoughts, but to go the extra mile and speak them out loud as personal confessions of faith.

- When you're not sure what decision to make, proclaim, "I know God will give me the wisdom I need!" (James 1:5)
- When the bills are piling up and the bank account is running low, proclaim, "I trust God. He will provide everything we need!" (Philippians 4:19)
- When other people are complaining about their jobs, reply, "Well, I'm glad I have a job. It may not be perfect but I am thankful for it!" (1 Thessalonians 5:18)
- When you're feeling tired and run-down, tell a friend, "I'm going to get some extra rest tonight, and I'm hopeful tomorrow will be a better day!" (Matthew 6:34; 11:28-29)

Anybody can spew negative words around, but that's why so many people are unhappy—they are doing what *anybody* can do. I encourage you to be one of the few people who speak out God's promises rather than rehearsing your problems repeatedly throughout the day.

It's this decision to speak positive, faith-filled words that will brighten your day and boost your own faith that God has better things in store.

Choose the Process of Change

Like many of the decisions we've talked about so far in this book, rejecting negativity doesn't come naturally for most of us…and it doesn't happen overnight. In fact, it takes a lot of practice. It's a process. There will be days that are challenging, but keep rejecting negativity and enjoy where you are, on the way to where you are going!

When I think about the process of personal change, I often think about Peter. God did quite a work in the life of Peter. Peter was transformed from a blunt, aggressive, mistake-prone fisherman into the preacher at Pentecost and a pillar of the early church. He made mistakes along the way—keeping the children from Jesus (see Matthew 19:14), taking his eyes off of Jesus and sinking in the water (see Matthew 14:30), resorting to violence (see John 18:10), denying he knew the Lord (see Luke 22)—but he learned through each of them. Peter didn't give up; he allowed God to change him. But it didn't happen in one day...one month...or even one year. It was a process.

When a baby is learning to walk, he falls many, many times before he gains the confidence to walk. Failing from time to time (which you *will* do) doesn't mean you're a failure; it means you're learning. It simply means that you don't do everything right all the time. But neither does anyone else.

> *Failing from time to time (which you will do) doesn't mean you're a failure; it means you're learning.*

If you've been accustomed to thinking and speaking negatively, the pathway to your freedom begins when you face the problem without making excuses for it. Embrace the process of change and be determined to learn something new about being positive each and every day. As you change your outlook from negative to positive, your words, actions, and attitude will change...and so will your life! This is one way to definitely make any day better!

Things to remember:

- We don't get to choose everything we experience on a given day, but we *do* get to choose how we *respond* to those experiences.

- Hope is a favorable and confident expectation; it's an expectant attitude that something good is going to happen and things will work out, no matter what situation we're facing.
- In your thoughts, your words, your actions, your attitude, your relationships—you can choose to be a positive person.
- A positive life is not only about thinking positive, God-honoring thoughts. It's just as important to speak positive, faith-filled words.

Suggestions for Putting "Reject Negativity" into Practice

- Think of things you refuse to let into your house: muddy shoes, flies and mosquitoes, pushy salespeople, and so on. Now add "negativity" to that list. Tell your family, "Negativity is no longer allowed in our house."
- Rather than dreading all the things that might go wrong, why not make a list of all the things you are hoping will go right today?
- Change is a process, but sometimes we can get discouraged when we think about how much further we have to go. As an exercise to encourage you, instead of looking at how much further you have to go, look at how far you've *already* come. Ten years ago, five years ago, five months ago—look at how far God has brought you!

CHAPTER 15

Be Patient with Yourself

Have patience with all things, but first of all with yourself.
—Saint Francis de Sales

I want to tell you a little story about "Beth." It's a story that might sound all too familiar. Beth is an adoring wife, a devoted mother to two growing teenagers, a full-time cashier at the local grocery store, and a faithful volunteer at her church. But Beth is having a rough morning (she often has these types of mornings). Let's look in and see what's going on . . .

"C'mon, guys! Hurry up! You're going to be late!" Beth shouted up the stairs. Picking shell pieces out of the egg yolks with one hand and pouring coffee with the other, Beth mumbled under her breath dejectedly, ". . . and *I'm* going to be late, too."

It was just another typical morning in the Connor house. Beth was running behind once again. Frustrated and annoyed with herself, she thought, *Why did I have to hit snooze that many times? I wanted to get up earlier today! I really wanted to spend time with the Lo—*

"Mom, the toaster's on fire!"

Beth turned to see Georgia, her sixteen-year-old daughter, racing toward the kitchen in alarm. Dropping her coffee, Beth darted to the pantry, searching frantically for the fire extinguisher. By the time she was back in the kitchen, extinguisher in hand, Georgia and her brother, Allen, had put out the small fire and were laughing hysterically at the burnt cinder that was supposed to be their morning toast.

Beth didn't have the energy to join in the merriment. Her nerves were shot. "Just get in the car—you'll have to find something to eat at school!" They loaded up the car and were halfway to Thomas Edison High School when Beth dropped her head in disbelief.

"Uh-oh. What is it, Mom?" Allen asked.

"I forgot some paperwork I was supposed to bring in to work today. Ugh, I can't believe I did that!"

"It's okay. Shake it off, Mom," encouraged Georgia. "It's been a crazy morning. Just explain to the boss you were busy trying to burn the house down."

Again, Allen and Georgia had a good-natured laugh, but Beth wasn't joining in the fun. She felt like she was tied up in knots. She hadn't done anything right this morning...not one single thing. And her failure was all she could think about.

As the kids got out of the car, Beth offered a weak, absentminded "Have a good day," but her thoughts were elsewhere. *How could I have messed this morning up so badly? Why can't I be a better mother? The kids are late; I'm going to be late—I'm a total failure.* Tears poured down her face. *Another bad day...another day I have messed up.*

Beth's story is all too familiar. The details are different for each of us, but we can all relate to the frustration that Beth is facing— she's doing the very best she can, but she is devastated when she messes up or comes up short. She is usually patient with everyone around her...but she isn't patient with herself.

I believe being patient with yourself is a vital step to take if you want to make every day better. 2 Peter 3:9 says that God is

> If God is patient with you, you can follow His example and be patient with yourself.

"long-suffering (extraordinarily patient) toward you." That's great to know, but here is something else we should glean from that verse of Scripture: If God is patient with you, you can follow His example and be patient with yourself.

When God is doing a work in your life—leading you to forgive, rooting out bitterness, renewing your joy, changing your attitude, teaching you to live a healthy life, and so on—it takes time to accomplish all He wants to do. If you get impatient with Him or with yourself in the process, you're going to quit before you see the completion and reap the reward. Rather than get frustrated and discouraged when you make a mistake or when it's taking too long, you can actually be refreshed—you can rejoice in the fact that God is patient with you and be patient with yourself!

How and Why You Can Be More Patient with Yourself

It's nearly impossible to enjoy life when you're impatient with yourself. People who haven't learned to accept that they're imperfect, and that God's work in their lives is a process, tend to have more difficulty accepting and getting along with others. Our study of God's Word shows us clearly that we should be kind, patient, loving, and forgiving, and that we should make every effort to be at peace with people.

I personally spent years having a hard time getting along with people, until I finally realized through the Word of God how my difficulty with other people was actually rooted in my difficulties with myself. The Bible says a good tree will bear good fruit, and a rotten tree will bear rotten fruit (see Luke 6:43). Likewise, the fruit of our lives comes from the root within us. Because I had roots of shame, inferiority, rejection, lack of love and acceptance, and more, the fruit of my relationships suffered. However, once I had a revelation of God's unconditional love for me and began to accept myself, eventually these new roots grew to produce good fruit, and my relationships began to thrive.

The same is true in your life. When you do the hard work of learning to love the person God created you to be, to accept that God is still working in your heart, and to be patient with Him in the process, your relationships are going to improve. The better you feel about yourself, the better you'll feel about others.

> The better you feel about yourself, the better you'll feel about others.

Here are a few tips I believe will help you become more patient with yourself:

Never put yourself down by saying things such as, "I always get it wrong," "I'll never change," "I'm ugly," "I look terrible," "I'm stupid," or "Who could ever love me?" Matthew 12:37 says that *"by your words you will be justified…and by your words you will be condemned."* Proverbs 23:7 says that *"as [a man] thinks in his heart, so is he."* In other words, the way we talk and think about ourselves determines how we feel about ourselves.

Don't compare yourself with other people. God must love variety, because He created us all differently—all the way down to our fingerprints. You'll never become patient with yourself if you're trying to be like someone else. Other people can be a good example to you, but trying to handle a situation just like someone else can lead to frustration. You don't know what God is doing behind the scenes in other people. You don't know what they are going through when no one is watching. Rather than comparing yourself with someone else, ask God for the grace to be the person He created you to be.

See your potential instead of your limitations. I once heard that actress Helen Hayes was told early in her career that if she were four inches taller she'd be the greatest actress of her time. I've heard that her coaches even went about trying various methods of stretching her, but nothing made her taller. Rather than getting upset because she wasn't tall enough, the famous actress decided to concentrate on her potential. As a result, she was eventually cast as Mary, Queen of Scots—one of the tallest queens who ever lived.

God can work around your limitations. And in many cases, He can even use your limitations for His glory. Don't get caught up in what you "can't" do. Trust God and allow Him to work His plan, because nothing is impossible with God (see Luke 1:37).

Find something you do successfully, and do it over and over. A big part of being patient is being confident. David was confident as he waited to face the giant Goliath in battle. Why? Because he remembered the fights he had won before—he had killed a lion and he had killed a bear. His previous success gave him the confidence he needed.

If you spend your time doing things you're not good at, it'll frustrate you and cause you to feel defeated and unsuccessful. Anytime you're feeling impatient with yourself because you are struggling with something you're not very good at, do something you do well. It's a practical way to build your confidence and calm any feelings of uncertainty. When I spend my day writing, I feel happy, fulfilled, and satisfied at the end of the day because I am good at writing. But if I were to spend a day trying to plant a garden, I would feel like I had failed at it miserably. Guess what? I don't do gardening!

Rest in your uniqueness—have the courage to deal with criticism. One of the most critical things to remember in order to be patient with yourself is to be a God-pleaser, not a man-pleaser (see Galatians 1:10). If you dare to be different, you'll have to expect some criticism. Going along with the crowd—when you know in your heart God's leading you a different way—is one reason people are so miserable. People-pleasers live their lives trying to change themselves all the time to make somebody else happy. You won't enjoy your life very much if you go against your own convictions. Instead, follow what God has put in your heart and ignore the criticism of others.

Keep your flaws in perspective. People with a high level of confidence have just as many weaknesses as people without confidence, but they concentrate on their strengths, not their flaws or weaknesses. Just because you have a bad day, make a mistake, or fail to meet today's goal…don't get down on yourself. Keep it all in perspective. Look at the things you *did* get accomplished today. Look at how far God *has already* brought you. These things will give you proper perspective and a new level of patience moving forward.

A Prayer for Patience

I know that it's not easy to wait patiently for God to complete His work in your life. It's good that you *want* to improve—it's good that you *want* to change. Beth wanted to be a great employee and an even greater mother. It's good that she was trying her best and that she cared about being on time. But when she messed up, she compounded the problem by being self-critical and impatient with herself.

Don't make the same mistake Beth made. Give yourself a break when you make mistakes or fail at something. Your only other option is to give up on yourself and spend your life with someone you don't like, and that someone is you! Elbert Hubbard said, "How many a man has thrown up his hands at a time when a little more effort, a little more patience would have achieved success."[8]

Don't give up...you're improving every day, even if you don't feel that you are. Trust that God knows your heart and that He is going to bless your effort. If you'll relax and be more patient with yourself, you will enjoy each day more and more.

Let me close this chapter by giving you a sample prayer to pray if you feel like you need more patience:

> Father, I thank You that I am fearfully and wonderfully made. You created me, and You have a great plan for my life. Forgive my mistakes, my faults, and my failures. And help me to forgive myself. I realize that Your work in my life is a deep, long-lasting, healthy transformation. So let each day, and each new experience, be part of that work. I want to learn each day, and I want to grow closer to You in the process. Thank You for giving me the strength to do that. Amen.

Things to remember:

- When God is doing a work in your life—leading you to forgive, rooting out bitterness, renewing your joy, changing your attitude, teaching you to live a healthy life, and more—it takes time to accomplish all He wants to do.
- When you do the hard work of learning to love the person God created you to be, to accept that God is still working in your heart, and to be patient with Him in the process, your relationships are going to improve.
- The way we talk and think about ourselves determines how we feel about ourselves.
- You'll never become patient with yourself if you're trying to be like someone else.

Suggestions for Putting "Be Patient with Yourself" into Practice

- Write up three "Get Out of Jail Free" cards. Give them to yourself when you mess up in the future. You don't have to live in a jail of condemnation.
- The next time you are feeling overwhelmed or impatient with yourself, stop and count to twenty. Allow God to speak to you in those twenty seconds, reminding you to be patient with yourself.
- Write down your intentions—not your actions—for your life and those around you. That list describes what I call your "heart motives." You may not always be perfect, but God sees your heart. Ask Him to help you line up your actions with your intentions in the future.

CHAPTER 16

Receive and Give Grace

I am not what I ought to be, I am not what I wish to be, I am not what I hope to be, but by the grace of God, I am not what I was.

—John Newton

Several of Paul's letters to the churches begin with the greeting, "Grace and Peace be multiplied to you." That is not something we would likely say today to greet another person, but it is a powerful statement that we need to understand.

We all want peace, yet we cannot have it unless we understand grace. I tried for years to have peace with no success, and it was because the only thing I knew about grace was that I was saved by it!

> For by grace you have been saved through faith, and that not of yourselves; it is the gift of God, not of works, lest anyone should boast.
>
> Ephesians 2:8–9 (NKJV)

By God's grace, my sins had been forgiven, but I didn't understand that I needed the same grace for my daily living that I needed for my salvation. Receiving Christ as our Savior is one thing, but living for Him is quite another. It seemed to me that living the Christian life took a lot of work and effort, and no matter how hard I tried, I always failed. I was frustrated daily because I wanted to be what God's Word instructed me to be, and yet, I didn't seem to have the power to behave accordingly.

Talk about having a bad day! That was the story of my life! Then finally I saw it: God's Word teaches us to live for Jesus in the same way that we received Him (see Colossians 2:6). We are saved by grace, and we are to live by grace; if we don't, then we will never have any peace, and without peace we will never have joy!

Grace is defined as God's undeserved favor, and as the power and ability that is needed for us to do what He asks us to do. God would never tell us to do something and then leave us without the ability to do it. His grace saves us and then it carries us successfully through our journey with Him. Grace is available at all times, but it is received only through faith! In other words, we need to ask for it and trust that we have it as a gift from God.

> God would never tell us to do something and then leave us without the ability to do it.

My life was changed forever when I found out that God's grace would change me if I trusted Him for it, and it will do the same thing for you. Our testimony can be the same as John Newton's, depicted in the quote at the beginning of the chapter. We are not what we want to be, or what we wish we were, or hoped we were, but by the grace of God, we are not what we used to be. We are being changed into His image daily, by His grace.

Our part is to ask, to be patient, to study His Word and trust the inherent power in it to do its work! I am not suggesting there is no effort on our part to apply discipline to our behavior, but it must be a godly effort, not a fleshly one. It must be effort made in and by the Holy Spirit, not effort we make on our own, without asking for God's help.

Our Daily Struggles

You can get out of bed on any morning hoping things will go the way you had them planned, only to find out that that is not going to be your reality. By the time you are up thirty minutes, you have received a phone call telling you that the highway you travel to get to work is backed up for miles due to an accident. You think, *This is going to be a bad day.* But it doesn't have to be if you understand how to access God's grace. You can ask God to help you, to give you the grace to know the best way to handle the situation, and if you remain calm, it won't be long before you have assurance in your heart of how to handle the dilemma. You will think of a different route that you can take, or you can call the office and explain the situation and pray they will graciously understand. You have many options other than "having a bad day."

Grace will help you raise a special needs child. It will help you stick with a difficult marriage. It will help you continue ministering to others even when they don't seem to appreciate it. Grace will help you graduate from college even though learning is a bit difficult for you. And it will help you stay calm when the highway is backed up and you can't get to work on time. Grace is amazing, and yet it is practical. It comes from Heaven, and yet it works in our daily lives right here on earth!

There is no need we have that the grace of God cannot meet! It is what we need to live in peace and enjoy life!

Grace conquers our mountains. The prophet Zechariah told the people who were concerned about how they were going to finish the temple they had been instructed to build that they were to cry out, "Grace, grace to it" (see Zechariah 4:7). A mountain of human obstacles was in their way, but grace removed them all. Your mountains will also be moved by the grace of God if you will depend on God's power, rather than your own ability, to do what needs to be done.

Grace Becomes Gratitude

When we are fully aware that God continually gives us "undeserved favor," how can we respond in any way other than with gratitude? God wants us to be thankful, but we won't be if we think our good works earn God's blessings. Gratitude comes when we know we don't deserve the gifts we are given by God, but that He gives them anyway because He is good! Always remember that grace is undeserved favor and power, and it is available to you in whatever quantity you need. The Bible says in James 4:6 that we have grace and more grace to help us overcome our evil tendencies. Think about it: not just grace, but grace and more grace!

It feels good to be thankful instead of worried, and grateful instead of filled with fear. A thankful heart is a happy heart.

Grace Brings Us into God's Rest

The writer of Hebrews teaches us that we enter God's rest through believing (see Hebrews 4:3, 10). Entering God's rest is not a rest from our labor, but it is a rest *in* labor. Entering God's rest doesn't mean we go take a nap; it means we rest internally, no matter what is going on externally. We can do all we need to do, but we do it while simultaneously resting in God's grace. God's rest is truly a supernatural place that can only be understood by those who have experienced it.

Your circumstances say that you should be worried, anxious, and frantically trying to figure out how to solve your problems, but instead of doing any of that, you are calm, peaceful, and enjoying life! "How can you be this calm with your situation?" people may ask. And when they do, it is your opportunity to tell them about the goodness of God.

When we live in the rest of God, we will live longer! Rest brings a refreshing to our souls that is needed in order to maintain good health. People may give their bodies a vacation, without their soul ever going on vacation. You can be on the beach in the sun all day and worry all day also. That is not true rest! But you could work all day while being filled with peace, joy, and gratitude and be more rested at the end of the day than the person who went to the beach! Internal rest is a vital need that many people rarely experience, and it only comes from understanding and receiving the grace of God in all that we do.

Here are three ways we can recognize that grace is missing:

- When we feel frustrated, that means we are into what the Bible calls "works of the flesh," which happens when we try to do God's job, in our own energy, without Him. So when you feel frustrated, stop and immediately ask for grace and even more grace if needed. Receive it by faith and let God lighten your load.
- When we are exhausted and have a headache from worry, we desperately need to stop and ask for and receive grace. Grace leads us to peace, not to worry and exhaustion.
- When we feel like giving up, we need another dose of God's grace. His power enables us to keep going even when nothing seems to be happening.

These are just three symptoms of needing grace, but there are countless others. Basically, anything that makes us miserable is a sign that we need more grace to deal with daily life. Even if we are jealous of someone, we need God's grace to overcome that fleshly trait. I don't think I would be going too far to say grace is the answer to every problem, because grace is God in action!

Grace Makes Us Gracious

"Graciousness" is a word that is used in defining grace. It is God's graciousness toward us, and once we see the beauty of it, we eventually want to give it to others. Being gracious and merciful toward the people who hurt and disappoint us is one of the ways we can say "Thank You" to the Lord for His grace toward us.

How can we justify withholding love from the imperfect people in our lives, when God continues loving us even though we are imperfect? I don't think it is possible.

I struggled a lot trying to show love to people who were hard for me to love, but when I gave up merely *trying* and received a greater revelation of God's love for me, it began to flow out of me freely, instead of my trying to squeeze a little out to share with others. I encourage you to study and focus on God's love and grace toward you, and I can promise you that you will change. It won't necessarily all come quickly, but it will come little by little, and one day you will barely remember the person that you used to be...you know, the one you spent so many *bad days* with. We live with ourselves all the time, and when we are not receiving and giving grace, we are hard to live with!

The more gracious you are to others, the happier you will be. Give people grace, and when needed, give them more grace! Get grace flowing in your life. Receive it from God and give it away!

Receive more and give even more away! One of the best ways we can introduce people to Jesus who don't know Him is to show them grace and mercy when they know they deserve punishment or rejection. Will it be hard? Not if you remember that God gives it to you every day of your life!

Things to remember:

- We all want peace, yet we cannot have it unless we understand grace.
- Grace is available at all times, but it is received only through faith! In other words, we need to ask for it and trust that we have it as a gift from God.
- Grace is amazing, and yet it is practical. It comes from Heaven, and yet it works in our daily lives right here on earth!
- Internal rest brings a refreshing to our souls that is needed in order to maintain good health.

Suggestions for Putting "Receive and Give Grace" into Practice

- Anytime you feel frustrated, stop and ask God for grace instead of trying to keep going in your own strength.
- Make a list of the things that have frustrated you over the past several days. Now look at that list and contemplate how God's grace can change each of them and allow you to enjoy your day.
- In your busiest moments today, take a moment to remember you can be in God's rest no matter how busy you may be on the outside. Give your soul a vacation... even when your body is at work!

SECTION IV

Before It's Too Late

When you lie down, you shall not be afraid; yes, you shall lie down, and your sleep shall be sweet.

Proverbs 3:24

CHAPTER 17

Finish a Project

Well done is better than well said.

—Benjamin Franklin

This was it...this was the moment of truth. What would they do? What would his decision be? For weeks they had been ridiculed. Relentlessly, they had been taunted. But now...now it was getting dangerous. Their lives were being threatened. Now it was real. What decision would their leader, Nehemiah, make? This wall—the wall around Jerusalem—was important, but was it really worth fighting for? Dying for? Maybe they should just pack up and go home. What would Nehemiah's orders be?

I wonder what the people felt in Nehemiah chapter 4 as they awaited Nehemiah's decision. Were they nervous? Afraid? Or were they determined and ready to fight? These men, women, and children weren't warriors, after all. They were construction workers. They had come with Nehemiah to rebuild the wall around Jerusalem that was lying in ruins.

But along the way, Nehemiah and his group of dedicated craftsmen came up against opposition. The enemies of Judah on all sides were "angry" that the wall was being rebuilt and they "ridiculed" the Jews as they constructed the wall (see Nehemiah 4:1–3). The mockery didn't work, though—Nehemiah instructed the people to keep building. And this is when things got danger-ous. Nehemiah 4:11 says:

> And our enemies said, "They will not know or see till we come into their midst and kill them and stop the work."

So this is where we pick up the story. Will Nehemiah quit? Will they leave the project unfinished? Will fear and opposition cause them to give up on the thing God put in their hearts to do?

I'll let Nehemiah tell you in his own words. He says in Nehe-miah 4:15–18:

> And when our enemies heard that their plot was known to us and that God had frustrated their purpose, **we all returned to the wall, everyone to his work.**
>
> And from that time forth, half of my servants worked at the task, and the other half held the spears, shields, bows, and coats of mail; and the leaders stood behind all the house of Judah.
>
> Those who built the wall and those who bore burdens loaded themselves so that **everyone worked with one hand and held a weapon with the other hand,**
>
> And every builder had his sword girded by his side, and so worked. And he who sounded the trumpet was at my side.

Rather than quit and go home, Nehemiah and his followers decided to finish the task. They were so determined to rebuild the wall around Jerusalem that, when facing danger, they worked with one hand and carried a weapon in the other. What a powerful picture of determination! They didn't let ridicule, intimidation, or danger slow them down. These men and women of God were determined to finish what they had started!

Seeing It Through

Have you ever started something and not finished it—a project, a goal, a dream? If you have, don't worry; you're not alone. I think we've all experienced the frustration and disappointment of unfinished plans at some point in our lives. The truth is, sometimes starting is the easiest part. However, I want to encourage you that with God's help, you can finish whatever you start. It doesn't matter who takes sides against you or what obstacles appear, if you'll be determined like Nehemiah, you're going to carry that thing through to completion, and God is going to be glorified.

How can this help you if you're having a bad day? It is possible that the reason you're having a bad day is because when you got up this morning, what you saw was unfinished projects, and your thoughts were about goals that you never completed. That can be very discouraging to anyone, but there is an answer. We need to be determined to be "finishers"! People who finish what they start, no matter how long it takes or how difficult it is.

I believe that when we feel a passion to do something, we should submit our goal to God, and then pursue it with all our hearts.

- If your passion is to sing, don't let one failed audition stop you. Keep learning, keep practicing, and pursue your dream. *Finish what you've started!*
- If your desire is to get your degree, don't let financial opposition stop you. Work hard, save up, and take one class at a time if you have to. *Finish what you've started!*

- If you've promised someone you will help them with a project, don't quit the moment it gets difficult. Be true to your word and see the project through. *Finish what you've started!*
- If you've determined you'll spend some time each day with the Lord, don't beat yourself up if you miss a day or if you fall asleep when you're supposed to be praying. Try again tomorrow. *Finish what you've started!*

Whatever it is that you are working on, or dreaming about, your life will be so much better if you will be determined to see it all the way through.

For example, I am passionate about teaching people the Word of God. That's because God spoke to me and put that desire in my heart. If I had gone and done something else instead, or if I had quit when things got difficult, I probably would have spent the rest of my life feeling frustrated and unfulfilled. That's what happens when we are passionate about a thing and we don't do something about it. Are you depressed or upset and having a bad day because you gave up on something you were supposed to do? The good news is that even when we're tempted to think that it's too late to start over, with God, it's never too late. Let me show you what I mean.

Back Up and Pick Up Where You Left Off

Years ago, at one of our conferences, a woman who was attending met several other ladies who shared their stories of past abuse and how they had overcome it. This really affected her, because she had a lot of trouble in her life from the abuse she'd experienced. By the end of the conference, she shared a great lesson she had learned.

"The other women at my table had been set free from their issues," she said, "but I was still dealing with mine—and now I realize why. God had instructed me to do many of the same things He had told the other women to do. The only difference was, they did what He asked them to do...and I didn't."

So let me ask you a question: Have you ever had the feeling God wanted you to do something or deal with something but you didn't fully obey? I have, and it's not a particularly good feeling. But when we find ourselves in a situation like that, there is a solution: We can back up and do what God told us to do or deal with the issue He wants us to deal with. In other words, we can still go back and finish what we've started.

The truth is, we will never experience the fullness of joy and freedom that's available to us in Christ if we refuse to complete what God calls us to do. It might be a huge thing, like starting your own business, or a small thing, like getting your home organized and in order. If it is in your heart, you won't be totally satisfied until you do it!

> We can still go back and finish what we've started.

Maybe there is someone in your life you need to forgive. Or you simply need to start eating right or be a better steward of your time, talents, and resources. Or maybe you're settling for less in a certain area of your life when God wants you to follow His plan to do something greater. Whatever it is, don't look back, only wishing you had obeyed God's voice—you can go back and start again. It's not too late to finish what you've started. With God's help, you are able to do everything He asks you to do. Just determine to be diligent and press on to do whatever it takes to get the job done right.

Anybody Can Start Something, But...

Many years ago I came across a verse of Scripture that caused me to weep before the Lord. In John 17:4 (NIV), Jesus says:

> I have brought you glory on earth by finishing the work
> you gave me to do.

Ever since reading that verse, it's become very important to me that I not just work at what God has called me to do, but that I *finish* what He's called me to do. There are a lot of people who step out and *begin* a thing—they start a ministry, they open a business, they begin a new diet, they start going to church, they begin a journey with God—but there aren't nearly as many who finish a thing.

Starting is an important first step. If God has put something in your heart to do, I strongly encourage you to start that thing in His timing. But it doesn't matter how many things you start if you never see them through to completion. This is why so many people are living miserable, frustrated, discouraged lives—they have yet to finish some things that God called them to do. The Apostle Paul said, *"If only I may finish my course with joy"* (Acts 20:24). He understood that there is great peace, great joy, and great happiness in completing what God has called you to do!

> It doesn't matter how many things you start if you never see them through to completion.

I'm determined to finish each thing I do! That's what I want for you, too. I want you to enjoy every single day of your life and finish what God has given you to do. From the smallest daily projects to the largest lifelong goals—I urge you to become a person who completes the task before you.

There is work to be done. We have a part to play...a big part. It's not all up to God. He has done His part and given us everything we need in Christ. It's up to us to keep learning, growing, and letting the Spirit of God work in us. Take time to consider the things that God has asked you to do and ask yourself, "What am I doing today to finish strong and complete what God has set before me?"

The Reward of Finishing Well

I'm happy to tell you that the end of Nehemiah's story is a happy one. Nehemiah's enemies never attacked—their threats were nothing but words. The wall was rebuilt and the splendor of Jerusalem was eventually restored. Upon completion of the wall, the prophet Ezra stood before the people and declared:

> Go your way, eat the fat, drink the sweet drink, and send portions to him for whom nothing is prepared; for this day is holy to our Lord. And be not grieved and depressed, **for the joy of the Lord is your strength and stronghold.**
>
> Nehemiah 8:10

Because Nehemiah and his followers were faithful to trust God and diligent to finish the task at hand, they experienced the joy that comes with a job well done! That's a joy you can experience, too. Whether it's finishing an unpleasant chore, completing an overdue assignment, being faithful to fulfill a promise, or accomplishing a lifelong dream, there is always joy in being able to say, "I did it!" And when you find yourself in those times when you don't know if you are going to make it—when the obstacles seem too big and the adversaries seem too threatening—don't give up; keep building that wall. It's a decision you'll never regret!

Things to remember:

- Don't let ridicule, intimidation, or any other obstacle slow you down. Be determined to finish what you've started.
- When you feel a passion to do something, submit your goal to God, and then pursue it with all your heart.
- There are a lot of people who step out and *begin* a thing, but there aren't nearly as many people who finish a thing.
- Take time to consider the things that God has called you to do and ask yourself, "What am I doing today to finish what God has set before me?"

Suggestions for Putting "Finish a Project" into Practice

- Find a craft, a chore, or a project around the house that you've left unfinished. Finish it today!
- Take a look at things you have failed to finish in the past. Now, ask yourself why you did so. Is there a common theme? Pray and ask God to give you the strength to finish well.
- Multitasking can be good, but don't let it be an excuse for working on several things at once but not completing any of them. The next project you start, see it all the way through to completion.

CHAPTER 18

Forgive and Forget

Forgiveness is the final form of love.

—Reinhold Niebuhr

Forgiving another person is something many people have a difficult time doing. If you've ever been badly hurt or deeply disappointed you probably know exactly what I mean. But I want to tell you about Erik Fitzgerald. I think his story is a great example for us to follow.

On October 2, 2006, Erik Fitzgerald's life was changed forever. That was the day he was informed that his wife, June, had been killed in a terrible car accident.

In the early hours of the morning, June was driving down a Georgia highway with their nineteen-month-old daughter, Faith, when a county EMS employee named Matt Swatzell collided with her car. Swatzell was just coming off of a twenty-four-hour shift and had fallen asleep at the wheel. Little Faith Fitzgerald survived the crash, but June and her unborn baby did not.

Erik Fitzgerald grieved the loss of his wife and their unborn child, but rather than be angry, hostile, or bitter with the man who took their lives, he did something else...he forgave him. Not only did he forgive Swatzell, but Erik developed a friendship with him. They started going to church together and occasionally shared a meal. As badly as he was hurting, Erik knew that Matt was hurting, too—dealing with tremendous guilt and sorrow. So Erik did what most people wouldn't do—he forgave. When asked by reporters how he could possibly have made the decision to offer such forgiveness, Erik Fitzgerald replied, "You forgive as you've been forgiven. It wasn't an option. If you've been forgiven, then you need to extend that forgiveness."[9]

What a powerful example of forgiveness! Erik was exactly right—we don't forgive because it's easy or because we feel like forgiving. We forgive because God first forgave us. The Apostle Paul said it this way in Ephesians 4:32:

> And become useful and helpful and kind to one another, tenderhearted (compassionate, understanding, loving-hearted), forgiving one another [readily and freely], as God in Christ forgave you.

But even though we've received God's forgiveness, and even though we know in our heart that we should forgive that person who hurt us or let us down, it can still be hard. If you really want to make each day better—if you really want to enjoy your life—it is important that you forgive those who have hurt or disappointed you.

This chapter is titled "Forgive and Forget" for a reason. You can stop rehearsing over and over in your thoughts all the details of what happened that hurt you, and you can forget about getting even. With God's help you can let go of all the bitterness, anger, and need to punish the person who wounded you. When you forgive them completely and trust God to handle the situation on your behalf—that is when you will become free to move on and enjoy the rest of your life. God is our Vindicator and He brings justice into our lives, but only if we let go of the offense and pray for those who have wounded us.

Forgiving Another Person Actually Benefits You

Many people ruin their health and lessen the quality of their lives by taking the poison of bitterness and unforgiveness. Matthew 18:23–35 tells us that if we do not forgive people, we get turned over to the "torturers." If you've held a grudge or harbored resentment in your heart, I'm sure you can agree. It's torture to have hateful thoughts toward another person rolling around inside your head. I can't even imagine how many bad days I have had in my lifetime simply because I was angry with someone who hurt or offended me. I refuse to live like that anymore and you can, too. We can choose forgiveness and enjoy every day of our lives.

Forgiving another person is of great benefit to…you! You're actually helping yourself more than the other person. I always looked at forgiving people who hurt me as being really hard. I thought it seemed so unfair for them to receive forgiveness when I was the person who had been hurt. I was in pain, but they got freedom without having to pay for the pain they caused. *Not fair!* But now I realize that I'm doing something healthy and helpful for myself when I choose to forgive.

When I forgive, I remove myself from the situation and allow God to do what only He can do. If I'm in the way—trying to get revenge or take care of the situation myself instead of trusting and obeying God—He has no obligation to deal with that person. However, God will deal with those who hurt us if we put them in His hands through forgiveness. The act of forgiving is our seed of obedience to His Word. Once we've sown our seed, God is faithful to bring a harvest of blessing to us one way or another.

There are still more ways that forgiveness benefits us:

- It releases God to do His work in the life of the person who hurt us, and to work in ours as well.

- We're happier and feel better physically when we're not filled with the poison of unforgiveness. (Serious diseases can develop as a result of the stress and pressure that bitterness, resentment, and unforgiveness put on a person.)
- Mark 11:22–26 clearly teaches us that unforgiveness hinders our faith from working. (The Father can't forgive *our* sins if we don't forgive other people. We reap what we sow. Sow mercy, and you'll reap mercy; sow judgment, and you'll reap judgment.)
- Your fellowship with God flows freely when you're willing to forgive, but it gets blocked by unforgiveness.
- Forgiveness also keeps Satan from getting an advantage over us (see 2 Corinthians 2:10–11). (Ephesians 4:26–27 tells us not to let the sun go down on our anger or give the devil any such foothold or opportunity. Remember that the devil must have a *foothold* before he can get a *stronghold*. Do not help Satan torture you. Be quick to forgive.)

For all these reasons and more, recognize that as difficult as it might be, forgiving the person or people who hurt or offended you is actually the very best thing you can do . . . for you. That's why I like to say it this way: Do *yourself* a favor and forgive!

Do the Unthinkable

When someone offends you or hurts your feelings, how do you respond? Do you let it steal your peace? Do you let their actions rob you of joy? Is it something that makes your emotions run wild?

The Word of God tells us what we should do when people hurt us (and it's a pretty shocking idea):

> But to you who are listening I say: Love your enemies, do good to those who hate you, bless those who curse you, pray for those who mistreat you.
>
> Luke 6:27–28 NIV

That's a radical idea, right? When someone hurts us, we're instructed by God to love our enemies. That is what Erik Fitzgerald did. He actually wanted to help the man who caused the accident that killed his wife and unborn child, not to spend his life feeling guilty and condemned because he had made a mistake. Wow! What a great example he is of true love.

If you thought that was radical, Luke 6:35 (NIV) goes even further. It says:

> But love your enemies, do good to them, and lend to them without expecting to get anything back. Then your reward will be great, and you will be children of the Most High, because he is kind to the ungrateful and wicked.

Wow! Not only are we to pray for our enemies, but the Bible instructs us to actually do something good for them! God knows that it's one thing to *say* you forgive someone, but when you start putting actions to your forgiveness, it becomes real. It becomes real for them…but more importantly, it becomes real for you. You probably won't be able to do it in your own strength, but with God's help you can "do good" to those who have hurt you.

> *It's one thing to say you forgive someone, but when you start putting actions to your forgiveness, it becomes real.*

Let's get practical about how to do this. If we have a coworker who gets the promotion that we've been believing God for, the minute we start to feel jealousy and envy, we could do something like give them a gift certificate to their favorite restaurant and congratulate them on their promotion. Actions like this—any practical way to "do good"—have tremendous power. When we do it, it breaks the power of the devil, because Romans 12:21 says that we overcome evil with good. I have learned this principle and it has been life-changing for me.

When we can look at people who've hurt us with compassion and pray what Jesus prayed—"Father, forgive them for they know not what they do"—there's a party that goes on inside of us. Luke 6:35 says that when we forgive, *"your recompense (your reward) will be great (rich, strong, intense, and abundant), and you will be sons of the Most High."* God will reward your willingness to forgive!

None of us know when we may need to forgive, so I think it is wise to be ready! Pray ahead of time and actually plan on forgiving anyone who hurts or offends you. Refuse to go to bed angry, or to waste your day being bitter.

Forgiveness Check

If someone has hurt you, don't spend the next ten years of your life hurting yourself by hanging on to that offense. Most likely, that other person isn't even thinking about you, while you dwell on the incident for years. That only hurts one person—you.

Forgiveness is a process. It's a daily decision. Don't be discouraged if you feel like you forgave someone yesterday but you have a feeling of anger or resentment toward them today. Just choose to keep walking in forgiveness. *Forgiveness is not a feeling, it is a decision about how we will treat those who have wounded us!* If you're

> *Forgiveness is a process. It's a daily decision.*

not sure whether you've really for-given someone or not, let me give you three identifying traits of forgiveness:

1. Forgiveness doesn't keep score.

In Luke 15:29, the elder brother of the prodigal son said, *"Look! These many years I have served you."* Peter wanted to know *how many times* he had to forgive someone (See Matthew 18:21). Unforgiveness is always looking at the score. But in contrast, 1 Corinthians 13:5 says, Love *"takes no account."* Love doesn't count up the evil done to it.

Back in the early days of our marriage, when Dave and I were having an argument or disagreement, I had a bad habit of bring-ing up stuff that happened years before, and Dave would say, "Where do you keep all that stuff?" What was I doing? I was keep-ing score. I was holding on to all my grievances, and every new thing Dave did wrong would get added to this list. It kept growing until it became a bitter giant in my heart. I can actually remember many years ago sitting down one day and making a list of all the things Dave had done that I didn't think were right. Not too long ago, I made a list of all the things he does right. It is no wonder I wasn't happy back then and I am very happy now! Anytime you are having one of those *bad days* we have been talking about, do a heart check and ask yourself if there is anyone you need to forgive.

Ask God to help you erase the scoreboard. Rather than hold-ing on to the pain and hurt of past offenses, choose to forgive and

> *There is no "winning" by keeping score… there is only losing.*

then let it go. There is no "winning" by keeping score… there is only los-ing. Choose to forgive and refuse to keep score.

2. Forgiveness doesn't complain.

Have you ever caught yourself thinking something like, *You never do anything for me?* This attitude only sees what others *aren't* doing and doesn't see what they *are* doing. God's Word clearly shows that we're not supposed to complain. And if you complain about some incident or offense, you won't get past it. Don't waste time by complaining. It won't bring you joy and will only keep you stuck in bitterness and resentment.

3. Forgiveness gives to those who have been the source of their hurt.

A person who has completely forgiven will be willing to give to a person who has hurt them. Recently I asked someone to do something for me and they simply said, "No, I am not able to do that." I was surprised and disappointed, but didn't think much about it after that. About two weeks later, I had a beautiful candlestick and candle that I had purchased, but it wasn't fitting into my décor, and as I was talking to a friend about who I might give it to, she suggested the person who had declined to help me. Out of my mouth came these words: "I'm not interested in giving it to her; she didn't help me when I asked her to!" I didn't even know I hadn't forgiven her for disappointing me, but when I listened to myself, I knew my heart wasn't right. I quickly repented and said, "Yes, please give it to her!"

The Beginning of a Better Life

Forgiveness is the first step to a better day and a better life. It doesn't mean you don't acknowledge your pain, and it doesn't excuse the person who hurt you. But if you choose to let go of your bitterness and anger, God will heal your pain, and He will deal with the people who have done you wrong.

If you want to make today better (and tomorrow...and the next day...and every day moving forward), be a forgiving person. Choose to forgive the offense and forget about trying to get even. Remember: You've been forgiven much—this is your chance to give that same gift of forgiveness to another.

Things to remember:

- We don't forgive because it's easy or because we feel like forgiving. We forgive because God first forgave us.
- Not only are we to pray for our enemies, but the Bible instructs us to actually do something good for them!
- Forgiveness doesn't keep score, doesn't complain, and isn't jealous.
- Forgiveness always comes with a reward!

Suggestions for Putting "Forgive and Forget" into Practice

- Make a new list: Instead of keeping a list of all the people who have wronged you, make a list of all the things God has forgiven you for.
- In your prayer time today, pray for the people who have hurt you. Pray that God will heal them, change them, and bless them.
- Go out and buy a card or a small gift for someone who offended you in the past. Give it to them as a demonstration that you've forgiven them and you're letting go of all bitterness or resentment.

CHAPTER 19

Be Grateful

When it comes to life, the critical thing is whether you take things for granted or take them with gratitude.
—G. K. Chesterton

I once heard a joke about gratitude that went something like this:

Two friends met for coffee one day, and one of the friends looked especially upset—he was on the verge of tears.

"What's the matter?" his friend asked. "Why are you so upset?"

"Well," the distraught man replied, "my aunt passed away three weeks ago and left me $25,000."

"Wow! That's a lot of money!"

"You haven't heard it all," interjected the upset friend. "Two weeks ago, a cousin on my mother's side of the family died and left me $80,000."

"I'm sorry for your loss," said the listening friend, "but once again, that's quite a bit of money."

"And last week . . . my grandfather passed away and left me half a million dollars."

"What? You've inherited so much! How can you be upset?"

"I'll tell you how I can be upset: This week . . . nothing!"

I think this joke is more true to life than most people would like to admit. The truth is that we've been blessed with so much, and yet we are often so ungrateful. We often concentrate on the things we don't have, rather than the things we *do* have. But gratitude is born out of a heart of recognition—a heart that understands how much it has received.

> Gratitude is born out of a heart of recognition—a heart that understands how much it has received.

I think it is safe to say that any day can be improved by gratitude. One of the main causes of "bad days" is that we get our focus on what we don't have, instead of keeping it on what we do have. We think of what people haven't done for us, instead of what they have done.

Most people would agree that we have a lot to be thankful for. After all, for people living in developed nations, our lives are often filled with conveniences that are easy to take for granted. Many people live in comfortable homes, wear nice clothes, and have reliable transportation. We have no shortage of clean water or healthy food. We have access to quality health care and education, and basically live a good life with a lot of freedom, safety, and security. It's very easy to take these wonderful blessings for granted—and sometimes get into the bad habit of focusing on what we don't have. But we need to remember that millions of people around the world live without the basic necessities of life.

I still remember when one of our sons went with an outreach team for a weekend to minister to the homeless. I knew he had been deeply impacted when he called me and said, "Mom, if I ever complain again, please punish me for being so ungrateful!" He was really upset about his previous lack of gratitude once he saw the conditions other people had to live in.

Think about this:

- Those without a place to live would love to have a house to clean, yet many homeowners complain about having to keep their house clean.
- A person without a car dreams of having transportation, while someone who owns a car is more likely to complain about the cost of gasoline and oil changes.
- Someone who is unemployed is desperate for a job, while many people in comfortable jobs are grumbling about having to stay twenty minutes late.
- A woman with an imperfect husband may complain about his faults, but a lonely woman would be happy to have someone to eat a meal with.

We should ask God to help us maintain a proper perspective because we have been given so much. We really do have a lot to be grateful for!

But the truth is that it is very easy to forget how blessed we are. We do it all the time. In the United States, Thanksgiving seems to be the one day out of the year that we remember, *Oh yeah, I've got a lot to be thankful for!* But even that day often turns out to be more about the turkey, dressing, and pies than about giving thanks. Maintaining an attitude of gratitude isn't easy—it is something we definitely need to do on purpose. With that in mind, let me give you three things you can do today that will help you enjoy each day with a grateful mind-set:

Develop an Attitude of Praise and Thanksgiving

Perhaps the best thing we can do throughout the day is praise God and thank Him while we go about our day. No matter what you're trying to build—your family, your marriage, your business, financial security, or even an exercise plan—you can thankfully praise God as you go through the day. Look around and it won't be long before you will find many things to give praise for. This morning when I got out of bed, I thanked God that I could walk! Get started early and keep it up all day.

We can even praise God during the seemingly insignificant events that fill our schedule—little things like getting dressed (thank God you have clothes to wear), driving to work (thank God for your car and your job), going to the grocery store (thank God you didn't have to grow your food), the ability to send emails (thank God it so convenient to communicate with people these days), and hundreds of other routine things we may take for granted each day. We spend the majority of our time doing these everyday ordinary things, so why not learn to appreciate them, enjoy them, and praise God while doing them?

Developing a heart of praise not only honors God…it's good for us! A. W. Tozer said, "Without worship, we go about miserable."[10] The solution to misery is simple—give God praise. When we praise God for His goodness, His blessings, and His many benefits, it brings us peace and fills us with joy. Praising God is a tremendous way to brighten every day.

At my conferences, I make sure to be in the service as soon as the praise and worship begins because I love to be in God's presence. In fact, before I speak to an audience, I make sure I have entered into praise and worship. I want to fix my thoughts on God, thank Him for what He's done in my life and for the words He's given me to speak, and I want to give Him praise for everything else He's going to do.

The truth is, God doesn't need our praise or approval. We don't have to thank Him in order to make Him happy, to satisfy a spiritual requirement, or to try to motivate Him to do something else

> *Giving thanks throughout the day is simply a way to show God how grateful we are for who He is.*

for us. Giving thanks throughout the day is simply a way to show God how grateful we are for who He is.

Praise is said to be a tale or narrative of something God has done! When we thank God for simple things, like hot and cold running water in our homes, we are telling a tale of something God has provided and declaring His goodness. It's a thankful-heart attitude that says, *I love You, Lord. I worship You. I recognize this blessing is from You.* Regularly giving thanks to God not only helps us fully realize how He's working in our lives, it also gives us a new perspective—our mind is renewed, our attitude is improved, and we are filled with joy (see Psalm 16:11).

Start a Gratitude Journal

Psalm 1:2 says that the righteous person *"meditates"* on the *"precepts, the instructions, the teachings of God."* How does he do that? By studying God's Word. In order to meditate on the Word of God, it is necessary to read and study it on a regular basis. This morning as I walked outside for exercise, I meditated on and confessed God's Word for over an hour and a half. I could only do that because I have taken time over the years to fill myself with God's Word. The longer I thought about God's Word and His promises, the more energetic and alive I felt. God's Word has power in it. It is the food that feeds our spirits and keeps them strong.

Along with the Word of God, another thing you can meditate (focus, concentrate) on is a list of the good things God has done in your life. A great way to do this is to start a "gratitude journal." This is just a journal you use to document the blessings of God that you are thankful for.

Many times we are frustrated and miserable over the course of the day because we think everything is going wrong. But the truth is many things have gone *right*, and we just didn't realize them... or we forgot about them already. If you make a conscious decision to look out for the good things each day so you can put them down in your gratitude journal, you'll have a much better day, and when you feel downcast, you can read your journal and recall all of the amazing things God has done in your life.

I encourage you to try and see how many blessings come your way over the course of a day. How high could that number go if you are truly being grateful for the little blessings and the big blessings? *Ten things? Twenty things? Thirty or forty things?* I think you'll be surprised how much you have to be grateful for once you start to write them down. Even if you only do something like this occasionally, it will be very good for you. God loves to bless you—I have a feeling He is going to fill up your gratitude journal in record time!

Verbalize Your Gratitude

When was the last time you gave someone a sincere "Thank you"? I'm not talking about just thanking the barista when she hands you your coffee or thanking the cashier for your change (though it's good to thank them, too). I'm talking about genuinely thanking the people in your life.

- Thank you, husband, for your hard work and love for our family!
- Thank you, boss, for the opportunity you have given me to work here.
- Thank you, friend, for hanging out with me tonight and being an encouragement to me on a regular basis!

- Thank you, employee, for the good job you do and the commitment you have to the company.

You might think, *Joyce, I shouldn't have to do that. The people in my life know how I feel.* They don't know unless you tell them... and even if they do know, thanking them is a great reminder.

I'll let you in on a little secret: Telling someone "Thank you" is as beneficial for you as it is for them because it develops in you an attitude of gratitude. When you make the choice to thank those in your life, you become acutely aware of how blessed you are. It's nearly impossible to be cranky, frustrated, and miserable if you've been thanking people all day for even the smallest things. "Thank you" is a selfless phrase that brings about significant progress in your life.

> *"Thank you" is a selfless phrase that brings about significant progress in your life.*

Let's Get Started

Each moment that we're given is a precious gift from God. We can choose to have a thankful attitude and live each moment full of joy, simply because God is good and He has given us much to be thankful for. Let's end this chapter by making it practical. Here is a list of things (big and small) that you can be thankful for today:

- Your family
- A roof over your head
- The clothes on your back
- The friendships in your life
- The trials God has brought you through
- A dream that came true

- A healthy body (Even if you are dealing with a sickness, or have pain right now, you can be thankful for the other parts of your body that are healthy.)
- Your job
- The gifts and talents God has given you
- Clean water
- The modern technology that you make use of each day
- The Word of God
- God's unconditional love for you

Your list can (and should) go on and on and on. I'm just giving you a few things to get you started. I encourage you to make your own list and add to it each day. It's one of the best things you can do if you really want to enjoy your life and make the most of every day God gives you. There is no downside to gratitude—it's one of the healthiest, most joy-filled attitudes you can have. So what are you waiting for? The best time to be thankful is always right now!

> There is no downside to gratitude.

Things to remember:

- We have so much to be thankful for. Be careful not to take your blessings for granted, such as a comfortable home, nice clothes, reliable transportation, clean water, healthy food, access to quality health care and education, freedom, safety, and security.
- Maintaining an attitude of gratitude isn't easy—it is something we definitely need to do on purpose.
- When we praise God for His goodness, His blessings, and His many benefits, it brings us peace and fills us with joy.

- We can choose to have a thankful attitude and live each moment full of joy, simply because God is good and He has given us much to be thankful for.
- Telling someone "Thank you" is as beneficial for you as it is for them because it develops in you an attitude of gratitude.

Suggestions for Putting "Be Grateful" into Practice

- Get a journal or notebook today so you can start your gratitude journal right away.
- Tell at least five people in your life how thankful you are for them. Give them a call, write them a note, or tell them face-to-face. They are going to be so blessed... and so are you!
- Try this experiment: For the next week, make the first sentence you utter in the morning and the last sentence you speak at night be a sentence of thankfulness. See how this new attitude of gratitude increases your peace and joy.

CHAPTER 20

Be Amazed

Happy the soul that has been awed by a view of God's majesty.

—A. W. Pink

In chapter 13, I talked about the importance of slowing down, living in "the now" and focusing on what you're doing. It is good to be focused on what you are doing, but we need to also be sure that we don't miss all of the amazing things going on all around us. We can't accomplish much in life without focus, but we can't enjoy much of life without living amazed! Don't keep your head down, focusing on what you're doing so much that you miss the miracle of the moment. Martha did that! In the Bible we are told a story about Jesus going to visit the home of Martha and Mary. Martha was so preoccupied with serving and making sure everything was just right for the visit that she missed the miracle of the moment! Jesus was in the house, and she had an opportunity to sit at His feet and be taught by Him, but she was frustrated because Mary wasn't helping her. Mary, on the other hand, was sitting at His feet, listening to Him. When Martha complained to Jesus, He told her she was overly concerned

> We can't accomplish much in life without focus, but we can't enjoy much of life without living amazed!

and anxious about too many things, and that Mary had chosen the better thing (see Luke 10:38–42). The work was important, but right at that moment, paying attention to Jesus was more important. Make

> *Make sure that you are not so busy being miserable that you miss the miracles all around you.*

sure that you are not so busy being miserable that you miss the miracles all around you.

I have the privilege of sitting by the ocean sometimes when I work on my books. I have had times when I have kept my head down for seven or eight hours and never looked up except to go to the bathroom. The sad thing is I had the ocean in front of me, but I never saw it simply because I was trying to reach a goal. I am not suggesting that we shouldn't reach our goals; I am a very goal-oriented person, but I have learned that I can take a few moments every hour or so and enjoy the view and the book will still get done. Actually, I think we have more creative energy to do whatever it is we are trying to do if we pause and give ourselves a few moments to be amazed!

I want to encourage you to reject "head down" living and choose to be amazed. That's the kind of life God wants you to live—awestruck, astounded, inspired, and amazed. The goodness of God and the splendor of His creation are all around you if you look. Just imagine how much better every day of your life would be if you chose to be amazed by:

- The majesty of a sunrise
- The warmth of a hug
- The birds that seem to sing all the time
- The healing properties of a good laugh

- The love in your spouse's eyes
- The creativity of your children
- The loyalty of a friend
- The blessings you experience each day
- The talent of an artist
- The colors in the sunset
- The presence of God

These are just a few of the amazing things that happen each day, and they are too wonderful to miss. If you really want to make each day better, one of the best things you can do is take time to consider the great things going on all around you...and be amazed.

Now, I admit, the things listed above are subject to change. Maybe they're not *always* so obvious. Sometimes clouds hide the sunrise, occasionally a friend disappoints, and there are certain days when the birds aren't singing as loudly as others. But that doesn't mean you can't live amazed. I want to share two things with you that will *never* disappoint—two things that can amaze you day after day if you will see them: (1) the greatness of God, and (2) the privilege of trusting God.

The Greatness of God

"Amazing grace, how sweet the sound..."

"How great Thou art..."

"Jesus, Jesus, Jesus—There's just something about that Name..."

"Praise God from Whom all blessings flow..."

You probably recognize these lyrics from a few of the classic old hymns of the church. Their words convey a certain wonder and amazement at the greatness of God. This kind of wide-eyed, jaw-dropping astonishment certainly inspires a hopeful, confident outlook on life.

Here's what Scripture says about the strength and power of God:

> The Lord reigns, He is clothed with majesty; the Lord is robed, He has girded Himself with strength and power; the world also is established, that it cannot be moved.
>
> Psalm 93:1

> Yours, O Lord, is the greatness and the power and the glory and the victory and the majesty, for all that is in the heavens and the earth is Yours; Yours is the kingdom, O Lord, and Yours it is to be exalted as Head over all.
>
> 1 Chronicles 29:11

> Thus says the Lord: Heaven is My throne, and the earth is My footstool. What kind of house would you build for Me? And what kind can be My resting-place?
>
> Isaiah 66:1

Wow! Our God is so powerful that He is "clothed" with majesty—the earth is His footstool! That's something to be amazed by! There is no person, no enemy, no power, and no force stronger than our God—and He loves you!

> *There is no person, no enemy, no power, and no force stronger than our God—and He loves you!*

Today we have numerous ways to recognize and learn about God's greatness. We can watch and listen to Bible teachings on TV, radio, and the Internet; we can find encouragement through social media; we can listen to uplifting music; we can read helpful, Bible-based books...the list is almost endless. But sadly, even with all of these ways to be amazed, it still seems that a lot of our reverence and awe of God is lacking.

Familiarity may be the main reason we've lost our sense of awe about Who God is. When we allow something—or someone—to become common or ordinary to us, we can often begin to take it for granted and it is no longer special. For many people, this is what has happened with their view of God.

This is what happened to the children of Israel in the first book of Samuel. The Ark of the Covenant was extremely important to the Israelites because it contained the presence of God. It was holy and revered. It was special...so special it was not to be touched by human hands. The priests inserted poles through rings on its sides in order to carry the Ark because no one was permitted to touch it. The presence of God was sacred to them. The Ark went before them everywhere they went. They even followed it into battle—and when they did, they won every conflict!

Amazing, right? The greatness of God was truly something to be amazed by!

But look at what happened: Rather than stay amazed, the Israelites began to get too familiar with the presence of God. They began to take Him for granted, and when they did, their enemies began defeating them in battle. The Philistines actually took the Ark away from them. They lost the presence...the glory of God! And even when they eventually got the Ark back, some still didn't treat it respectfully, touching it, even though they were forbidden to do so (see 1 Samuel 4–6).

If you feel like you've lost your sense of awe, don't worry—you can stir it up again. Our perspective of God is sometimes like a jar of salad dressing sitting on a shelf—most of the seasoning settles to the bottom of the bottle, but when you shake that bottle up, all the ingredients mix together and then the dressing can add flavor to a salad. In the same way, we can stir ourselves up and regain the wonder, reverence, and awe we once had for the Lord. I have to do this from time to time. We can all get so entrenched in living life and dealing with our daily issues that we forget how amazing God is. Stir up those memories of what God has done for you. Begin to do what you did when you were first filled with God's presence, His grace and love. I can promise you that God is doing amazing things every day around you and for you, but you may just need to take time to recognize them. The more amazed you are, the better each day will be!

There are several ways we can stir ourselves up. Just stop and think for a moment:

- Begin to reminisce about the goodness of God in your life. Remember things He's already done to bless you.
- Consider some of the bad situations He has protected you from. Perhaps you missed a bad accident because you locked your keys in the car and ran late for work. Things like this are not necessarily coincidences, and we are able to see the hand of God at work in them if we simply pay attention.
- Keep a journal to record your prayer needs and then the answers and breakthroughs, or a gratitude journal to write down things you are thankful for.
- Share with others what God is doing in your life! It doesn't matter whether they're big or small things; remembrance is vital to maintaining hope, and these things can help remind you.

When you focus on how awesome God is—and all the great things He *has* done, *is* doing, and even *will* do in your life—your natural response will be to be amazed! Don't allow yourself to ever get accustomed to the love and mercy of God in your life—they are great blessings and they are enough to keep us amazed for as long as we live.

The Privilege of Trusting God

Over the course of this book, I've talked about a lot of different ways to help you enjoy the life Jesus came to give you. We've covered topics as practical as time management and as profound as trusting God in every situation in life.

God wants to help us...He loves us...we are His children. But He will not force His help on us at any time. He sees us when we struggle our way through things, and I am sure it makes Him sad, because all we have to do is ask Him for help. God taught me this truth in a way I'll never forget.

My husband, Dave, is tall. And I...well, I'm not so tall. We have a really high window over the kitchen sink in our house. When that window is open, there's no way for me to close it without going through a big ordeal. But how do you think it would make Dave feel if I ran out of the house to go ask the man next door to come and close that window for me? Or what if I tried to do it myself, straining and stretching, maybe climbing up on the counter, possibly knocking things over, getting all worn-out—when all the while Dave was sitting right there? That would really be insulting to him.

In the same way, how do you think it makes God feel when He sees us running to others for help or struggling on our own so needlessly? I think He is grieved, because He doesn't want to see His children hurting. With any issue you face, God is right there waiting for you to simply *ask for help.*

So whatever changes you have been inspired to make throughout the pages of this book, the process to a new, better, more enjoyable life is simple: (1) Humble yourself, (2) trust God and ask for His help, and (3) then do whatever He may ask you to do. When you follow these simple steps, you'll be amazed at how much better life can be.

We often look at trusting God as something we need to do, or have to do, but in reality, the invitation to trust God is a great privilege and something that certainly should amaze us. I'm amazed that I have God on my side, and He can do anything, anywhere, because nothing is impossible for Him. I am sure you feel the same way, or you will if you take time to think about it.

You are not alone, you are not without help, God has a plan, and even if you have sinned, He will cleanse you and help you without reproach or fault-finding. You have the great privilege of taking any problem to Him at any time, knowing that He listens, He cares, and He is ready to help!

There have been many times in my life when I've had a problem and I've said, "Well, I have done everything I know to do. I guess all I can do now is trust God." Perhaps you have said the same thing. That actually is a terrible statement and shows how little faith we often have. Let us now say, "I have a problem and I am blessed to be able to trust God to help me with it. I cast my care on Him, and He cares for me. I will wait on Him, and do anything He shows me to do, and I will trust Him for the strength and ability to do it."

Our bad days will be short-lived as soon as we learn to trust God in every situation and to do so without delay! We may have difficulties, but our hope and faith in Him will be more than enough to get us through them and to help us come out of them in total victory!

So lift up your head today and smile. God is amazing and He is your God!

Things to remember:

- Awestruck, astounded, inspired, and amazed—that's the kind of life God wants you to live.
- There are two things that can amaze you day after day if you will see them: (1) the greatness of God, and (2) the privilege of trusting God.
- When you recognize God for Who He is, you'll realize what He can do in your life.
- Trusting God is a privilege, not an obligation.
- God wants to help us…He loves us…we are His children. All we have to do is ask.

Suggestions for Putting "Be Amazed" into Practice

- Go outside and purposely look for at least three things God has created or given you that are "amazing." Stop what you are doing and thank Him for each of these things.
- Do a Bible study, finding Scriptures that describe the power, splendor, and majesty of God. Write down a few of these and post them on your refrigerator or another place where you'll see them often. Allow them to constantly remind you of the awesome greatness of God.
- Make a list of the things from this book you want to do in order to "make every day better." Now, before you do anything else, ask God to help you do it in *His* strength, not in your own.

NOTES

1 John Maxwell, *Your Road Map for Success Workbook: You Can Get There from Here* (Nasvhille: Thomas Nelson, Inc., 2006), 52.

2 "It Was Christmas Eve, 1910," SermonCentral, November 2006, http://www.sermoncentral.com/illustrations/sermon-illustration-warren-lamb-stories-29696.asp.

3 "Learning," Sermon Illustrations, http://www.sermonillustrations.com/a-z/l/learning.htm.

4 Dwight L. Moody, Brainy Quote, http://www.brainyquote.com/quotes/quotes/d/dwightlmo390829.html?src=t_little_things.

5 "Truth," Sermon Illustrations, http://www.sermonillustrations.com/a-z/t/truth.htm.

6 "I have a choice about today," A Gift of Inspiration, http://www.agiftofinspiration.com.au/stories/attitude/Choices.shtml.

7 Samuel Smiles, Brainy Quote, http://www.brainyquote.com/quotes/quotes/s/samuelsmil143145.html?src=t_hope.

8 Elbert Hubbard, Brainy Quote, http://www.brainyquote.com/quotes/quotes/e/elberthubb391598.html?src=t_patience.

9 Ryan Blackshere, "Widower forges friendship with man in crash that killed wife, unborn baby," Today.com, February 3, 2014, http://www.today.com/news/widower-forges-friendship-man-crash-killed-wife-unborn-baby-2D12044681.

10 "Great Quotes on Worship," Experiencing Worship, September 24, 2013, http://www.experiencingworship.com/worship-articles/general/2001-7-Great-Quotes-on.html.

Do you have a real relationship with Jesus?

God loves you! He created you to be a special, unique, one-of-a-kind individual, and He has a specific purpose and plan for your life. And through a personal relationship with your Creator—God—you can discover a way of life that will truly satisfy your soul.

No matter who you are, what you've done, or where you are in your life right now, God's love and grace are greater than your sin—your mistakes. Jesus willingly gave His life so you can receive forgiveness from God and have new life in Him. He's just waiting for you to invite Him to be your Savior and Lord.

If you are ready to commit your life to Jesus and follow Him, all you have to do is ask Him to forgive your sins and give you a fresh start in the life you are meant to live. Begin by praying this prayer...

Lord Jesus, thank You for giving Your life for me and forgiving me of my sins so I can have a personal relationship with You. I am sincerely sorry for the mistakes I've made, and I know I need You to help me live right.

Your Word says in Romans 10:9, "If you declare with your mouth, 'Jesus is Lord,' and believe in your heart that God raised him from the dead, you will be saved" (NIV). I believe You are the Son of God and confess You as my Savior and Lord. Take me just as I am, and work in my heart, making me the person You want me to be. I want to live for You, Jesus, and I am so grateful that You are giving me a fresh start in my new life with You today.

I love You, Jesus!

It's so amazing to know that God loves us so much! He wants to have a deep, intimate relationship with us that grows every day as we spend time with Him in prayer and Bible study. And we want to encourage you in your new life in Christ.

Please visit joycemeyer.org/salvation to request Joyce's book *A New Way of Living*, which is our gift to you. We also have other free resources online to help you make progress in pursuing everything God has for you.

Congratulations on your fresh start in your life in Christ! We hope to hear from you soon.

JOYCE MEYER is one of the world's leading practical Bible teachers. Her daily broadcast, *Enjoying Everyday Life,* airs on hundreds of television networks and radio stations worldwide.

Joyce has written more than a hundred inspirational books. Her bestsellers include *Power Thoughts, The Confident Woman, Look Great, Feel Great, Starting Your Day Right, Ending Your Day Right, Approval Addiction, How to Hear from God, Beauty for Ashes,* and *Battlefield of the Mind.*

Joyce travels extensively, holding conferences throughout the year and speaking to thousands around the world.

Joyce Meyer Ministries
P.O. Box 655
Fenton, MO 63026
USA
(636) 349-0303

Joyce Meyer Ministries—Canada
P.O. Box 7700
Vancouver, BC V6B 4E2
Canada
(800) 868-1002

Joyce Meyer Ministries—Australia
Locked Bag 77
Mansfield Delivery Centre
Queensland 4122
Australia
(07) 3349 1200

Joyce Meyer Ministries—England
P.O. Box 1549
Windsor SL4 1GT
United Kingdom
01753 831102

Joyce Meyer Ministries—South Africa
P.O. Box 5
Cape Town 8000
South Africa
(27) 21-701-1056

100 Ways to Simplify Your Life
21 Ways to Finding Peace and Happiness
Any Minute
Approval Addiction
The Approval Fix
The Battle Belongs to the Lord
Battlefield of the Mind*
Battlefield of the Mind for Kids
Battlefield of the Mind for Teens
Battlefield of the Mind Devotional
Be Anxious for Nothing*
Being the Person God Made You to Be
Beauty for Ashes
Change Your Words, Change Your Life
The Confident Mom
The Confident Woman
The Confident Woman Devotional
Do Yourself a Favor...Forgive
Eat the Cookie...Buy the Shoes
Eight Ways to Keep the Devil Under Your Feet
Ending Your Day Right
Enjoying Where You Are on the Way to Where You Are Going
The Everyday Life Bible
Filled with the Spirit
Good Health, Good Life
Hearing from God Each Morning
How to Hear from God*
How to Succeed at Being Yourself
I Dare You
If Not for the Grace of God*
In Pursuit of Peace
The Joy of Believing Prayer
Knowing God Intimately
A Leader in the Making
Life in the Word
Living Beyond Your Feelings
Living Courageously
Look Great, Feel Great
Love Out Loud
The Love Revolution
Making Good Habits, Breaking Bad Habits
Making Marriage Work (previously published as *Help Me—I'm Married!*)
Me and My Big Mouth!*
The Mind Connection*
Never Give Up!
Never Lose Heart

* Study Guide available for this title

BY DAVE MEYER

Life Lines